T5-CGB-854

Words of Praise for
Spend Less, Sell More

"David Rosenzweig is the rare individual who is creative and practical at the same time. Readers of his new book will benefit from his keen ability to sift through the marketing hype and focus on the essentials that will help them analyze their individual situation and successfully integrate marketing into their day-to-day operations."

—Jan Eakins, Sales Communication Manager
Microsoft Corporation

"On target and a must read for any business wanting to grow in the competitive 90s. Companies need to realize the four traditional approaches to increasing revenue might have been the answer in the past but that the rules have now changed."

—Jim Fitzgerald, Senior Division Sales Manager
Boerhinger Mannheim Pharmaceuticals

"I think David Rosenzweig has identified and defined a marketing process that if applied can significantly help any company expand their business."

—Diane Solvang-Angell,
Communications Manager, Sales & Field Operations
Safeco Insurance Company

*Spend less-*SELL MORE

13 SIMPLE STEPS *you* can take right NOW *to* GROW *your* BUSINESS

DAVID ROSENZWEIG

PROBUS PUBLISHING

Chicago, Illinois
Cambridge, England

ISBN 1-55738-819-9

Printed in the United States of America

BB

CTV/BJS

1 2 3 4 5 6 7 8 9 0

To Karen for her honesty,
Shawna for her wisdom,
Allison for her joyfulness,
and to my parents
and sisters for their ongoing support.

CONTENTS

CONTENTS

PART 1

THE FOUNDATION

Introduction—What Is the Business Development Process?

The economic environment of the 1990s dictates the need to refine and redefine marketing strategies if a company is going to survive and prosper into the next decade. Common situations facing typical companies include increased competition, customers' requirements for lower costs and increased quality of product and services, shrinking budgets, and fewer resources for both venture capital and business loans.

In a nutshell, there is a greater need to increase revenue from new business and to lower overhead costs. An ever-increasing number of marketing professionals are being asked to bring in more sales dollars using less expense dollars. Companies from five employees to 1,000 employees are confronted with shrinking resources. Economic factors have forced downsizing of sales staff, operational staff, and administration staff.

How then, with fewer resources, does a company increase revenue? To increase sales a company could increase demand on salespeople, expand its salesforce, expand its advertising program, or increase the price of its product or service.

Each of these alternatives has a particular consequence attached.

Increase demand on salespeople. If your company has downsized, the sales staff is already spread thin. If the company has not downsized, pressure for increased sales has either already been applied, or the amount of increased revenue may not be great enough to make a large impact. Also, if your company's industry is like most, the realities of the economy are making it increasingly harder for sales professionals to just maintain their level of performance.

Expand its sales force. Expanding a company's sales staff is both expensive and a risky proposition (when taking into account costs of salaries, incentives, training, materials, and the amount of time necessary to bring new salespeople up to a break-even point).

Expand its advertising program. Expanding an advertising program may have a short-term effect, but the cost to reach an expanded audience and maintain that program may be too prohibitive for most business-to-business sales and service organizations.

Increase the price of its product or service. The least costly alternative, to raise prices, may be business suicide in an increasingly competitive economic world.

The alternative suggested in this book is the Business Development Process. The Business Development Process is based on the following:

- ➲ Efficiency

- ➲ Understanding the sales environment

- ➲ Precise targeting of markets

- ➲ Customer-driven comprehension of service or product benefits

- ➲ Setting up systems that can regularly be maintained through a quality management system

- ➲ Integrating marketing and sales resources to create new long-term customers.

Throughout the 1980s, management consumed a host of books on business theory, management technique, and sales philosophy. From excellence to quality, from building relationships to managing in one minute, each author gave business leaders mountains of information that have changed behavior and led to success stories for many companies.

4

In a fast-paced, expanding economy, those philosophies helped companies take advantage of the business environment of the last decade. Companies were expanding at will; new services and products were being developed almost overnight. Venture capital and cash to expand were easily available. Fueling this environment was a large number of customers who were eager to buy. Whether these services and products met the customers' needs was not a major concern to the companies providing these services and products. The market was there, and sales dictated the status quo.

In the current decade, a no-growth or slow-growth economy has created stiff competition for most service and product providers. Since customers now have many choices to make in selecting a service or product provider, companies need to satisfy the exact needs of the customer in order to compete.

In order to be successful in this environment, companies must have a process that maximizes current resources while targeting, penetrating, and—most importantly—gaining new customers. That is precisely the purpose of this book. The following pages present a practical system for small- to medium-sized companies to develop new business, utilizing a minimal budget to integrate marketing and sales through a program that will expand sales revenue.

The process is not magic. It requires well-planned, well-organized, and consistent work. It is a workbook that gives a philosophy; but more importantly it gives the procedures for utilizing existing tools, creating new tools, and developing a practical system to follow. The end result will be increased sales revenue.

This book is in seven parts.

Part I introduces preliminary concepts that are the foundation for the Business Development Process and explains how the thirteen-step Business Development Process works. The concept of analyzing the various aspects of your company's distinctive capabilities, your target market's characteristics, and your competition's ability to compete against your company, is presented. The objective of Part I is to give your company an overview of the entire process and to find an area where your company fits the target market's needs better than your competition.

Part II defines the elements and benefits of integrated marketing and sales functions. In addition, it discusses resources necessary to operate the system.

Part III begins detailing the first five steps in the Business Development Process. Beginning with targeting prospective customers within selected industries, your company learns the techniques of developing two-way exchange of information: educating prospective customers to your company's distinctive capabilities, while gaining an understanding of the prospective customers' needs and requirements.

Part IV discusses methods for communicating with prospective customers in the next four steps of the Business Development Process. The first objective is to use general information to build your company's name awareness. The second, based on what your company has learned about the prospective customer's needs and service requirements, is to use specific information to build knowledge of your own company's distinctive capabilities. Third, your company determines the perceptions of the prospective customer and identifies strategic business opportunities. Finally, your company demonstrates proof that there is a fit between your company's distinctive capabilities and the needs and service requirements of your prospective customer.

Part V focuses on the two steps of the Business Development Process that create a tactical plan to gain the prospective customer's business. Using the information generated from the two-way exchange of information, your company develops a solution to exactly meet the prospective customer's needs and service requirements. Then the solution is incorporated into a tailored proposal.

Part VI details the final two steps of the Business Development Process. The first objective is to present the proposal and gain a commitment from the prospective customer as an approved vendor. Then your company will work with the new customer so it can actually experience the performance and fulfillment of the commitments made in the proposal. The second objective is to cement a long-term relationship as the preferred vendor by continuously adjusting service and product solutions to maintain a value-added benefit to the customer.

Part VII outlines the necessary elements needed to set up a quality management system that will monitor, measure, and modify the Business Development Process.

To better gain an understanding of the steps that make up the Business Development Process, let's begin with an overview of how the process works.

The Business Development Process

Elements of the Business Development Process Model

The Business Development Process defines a set of action steps that are necessary to grow your business. The model we will build defines a target market, provides information that is important to the customer, and integrates marketing and sales resources strategically into a process plan. The result is a step-by-step practical system that uses the two-way exchange of information to maximize marketing and sales efforts. Smart marketing, smart sales.

Fit/Misfit Model

Prior to the first step of the Business Development Process, you must clearly define your company's distinctive capabilities, your target market's characteristics, and your competition's distinctive capabilities. This preliminary exercise will compare how each of these components match up, producing a fit/misfit model of the environment in which your company competes. Your staff will use this model to identify prospective customers in your company's target market. With each step of the Business Development Process, the number of prospective customers whose needs and service requirements fit your company's distinctive capabilities will decrease. At the same time, the fit between your company and the remaining prospective customers will become tighter. The outcome of this process maximizes the use of marketing and sales resources, while producing long-term profitable business relationships.

THIRTEEN-STEP BUSINESS DEVELOPMENT PROCESS

We can use a bull's-eye target to illustrate the thirteen-step Business Development Process. The target consists of four concentric rings, each representing a group of the thirteen steps. As we move step-by-step through the Business Development Process, prospective customers move toward the center of the target (see Figure 2–1).

Prospective customers at the outer edge of the target are groups of undefined target markets. Prospective customers that move further into the center will become more defined through the exchange of information. As the group of prospective customers moves further within the target, those that do not fit will drop out. More specific sales strategies will be developed to gain the business of those that do fit. As this group reaches the center its members have become actual customers. The process concludes with actions that will lead to long-term relationships with your new customers.

THE OUTER RING OF THE
BUSINESS DEVELOPMENT PROCESS TARGET Model

The outer ring of the target model consists of the first five steps of the Business Development Process. These steps determine which prospective customers within the target market will be pursued by gathering the necessary information about the prospective customers, as well as beginning the preliminary flow of information to and from the target prospect group.

Step 1 **Target:** Identify the prospective customers in the target market groups to be pursued. Obtain addresses and phone numbers of headquarters location via research.

Step 2 **Identification:** Identify the decision maker for each prospective customer. This information can be gathered by research or by phone interview.

FIGURE 2–1   THE THIRTEEN STEPS IN THE BUSINESS DEVELOPMENT PROCESS THAT MOVE A PROSPECT TO CENTER

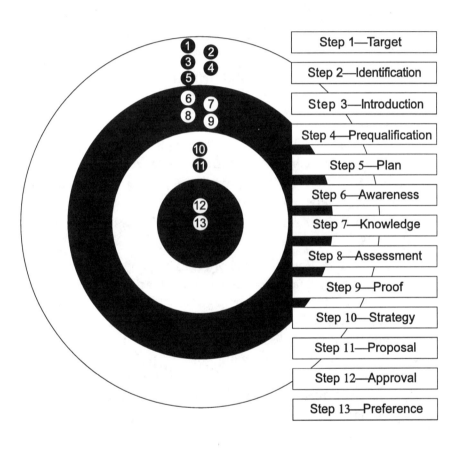

Step 1—Target

Step 2—Identification

Step 3—Introduction

Step 4—Prequalification

Step 5—Plan

Step 6—Awareness

Step 7—Knowledge

Step 8—Assessment

Step 9—Proof

Step 10—Strategy

Step 11—Proposal

Step 12—Approval

Step 13—Preference

Step 3 **Introduction:** Introduce your company to the target prospect group. In most cases, this will take place via letter and brochure.

Step 4 **Prequalification:** Assess preliminary needs and identify competitors. Gather this information through surveying prospective customers.

Step 5 **Plan:** Develop a strategic plan for account-specific marketing communication. Determine specific marketing communications, and implement a schedule.

The Outer-Middle Ring of the Business Development Process Target Model

The outer-middle ring of the target model consists of the next four steps of the Business Development Process. These four steps produce the major two-way exchange of information that educates the prospective customers within the target prospect group about your company's distinctive capabilities. This two-way exchange of information also educates the company about the needs and service requirements of the target market.

Step 6 **Awareness:** Raise the level of your company's name awareness to the target prospect group. This is accomplished through direct mail.

Step 7 **Knowledge:** Develop prospective customer's knowledge of your company's distinctive capabilities. This is accomplished by customized direct mailings or sales presentations.

Step 8 **Assessment:** Learn prospective customer's perception of your company. Identify specific business opportunities. This is done primarily by phone or in person through your company's salesforce.

Step 9 **Proof:** Based on prospective customer's requirements, submit information that demonstrates proof of your company's capabilities. This can be accomplished either in a live presentation or in a tailored mailing.

THE INNER-MIDDLE RING OF THE
BUSINESS DEVELOPMENT PROCESS TARGET MODEL

The inner-middle ring of the target model consists of the next two steps of the Business Development Process. The two steps of this stage of the process are critical. Plans must be carefully developed and deployed. The objective of these two steps is to gain agreement by the prospective customer, that a good fit exists between your company's distinctive capablities and the prospective customer's needs and service requirements.

Step 10 **Strategy:** Develop a term-based sales strategy. Include marketing personnel, sales management, operations personnel, and field sales on your business development team. In a small business, this team may include one, two, or three individuals who perform multiple functions.

Step 11 **Proposal:** Develop and present a tailored sales proposal. Using your business development team of relevant personnel would facilitate this step.

THE CENTER OF THE
BUSINESS DEVELOPMENT PROCESS TARGET MODEL

The center of the target model consists of the final two steps of the Business Development Process. Within these two steps, your company will develop a closer relationship with the customer by monitoring how well needs and service requirements are met. First the prospective customer purchasing your company's service or product. Then your company will continue the process by taking the necessary actions to improve performance. This is the basis for a long-term relationship with your company designated as the primary supplier.

Step 12 **Approval:** Gain commitment from the prospective customer to use you as a supplier of service or product. Your company begins a continuous monitoring program of the customer's needs and service requirements.

Step 13 **Preference:** Your company is selected as the primary supplier of the service or product. Begin instituting a performance assessment program.

SUMMARY

The Business Development Process model is a defined step-by-step series of actions that combine integrated marketing and sales resources. This process strategically allows for the two-way exchange of information. The result is the education of your company, in which your staff learns the needs and requirements of the targeted prospective customer. At the same time, the targeted prospective customer learns of the distinctive capabilities of the service or product your company provides. The customer-driven model maximizes the efforts of your marketing and sales resources. The thirteen-step process uses fewer conventional resources to gain a significant increase in new business.

The thirteen-step process is built on the foundation of a clear definition of your company's distinctive capabilities, your target markets characteristics, and your competition's distinctive capabilities. Your staff will define the business climate your company works in with a fit/misfit model. The target prospect group within your target market will become more and more refined as the prospective customers move through each series of steps toward the center of the bull's-eye target model. Through the strategic exchange of information, prospective customers progress through the steps that make up the Business Development process. Prospective customers whose needs and service requirements fit your company's distinctive capabilities progress toward the center of the target, and your company develops more specific sales strategies. Prospective customers at the center have become customers, and your company takes the final two steps that will lead to long-term relationships.

Defining the Target Market: The Fit/Misfit Model

This chapter will show how to clearly define your target market by developing a model that illustrates how prospective customer's needs and service requirements and your company's distinctive capabilities fit or do not fit. The following three chapters will go into detail of the three elements that make up the model: distinctive capabilities, target market characteristics, and the competitor's distinctive capabilities. Once the fit/misfit model is developed, the Business Development Process can become a two-way education process.

Understanding Your Distinctive Capabilities

To begin developing your own model, your company must understand how customers perceive the capabilities that distinguish your company from competitors. This will become a customer-driven description of your company's distinctive capabilities defining what your company does, what it does well, what the industry's customers think of your company, how well your company meets the requirements of the industry's customers, and how your company's service performance has led to long-term customer relationships. This description will paint a picture of your company in the marketplace. Without this clear picture of your company's distinctive capabilities, your company will be unable to use its marketing and sales staff to inform prospective customers of your company's ability to provide a service or product.

But that is only part of the picture. Not having a clear picture of the characteristics of your target market is like driving a car down a road in a fog so dense you cannot see the terrain ahead of you. You need a map that reveals the characteristics of the industry's customers.

Understanding Your Target Market Characteristics

Describing the requirements shared by companies in your customers' industry will give you a clear picture of your target market characteristics. This picture will illustrate how well your company's service or product meets the needs of the industry's customers, how your industry's customers choose price versus a service or product feature in making a purchasing decision, how your location or your distribution channels define your market, who the competition is, and what the current situation is that dictates the conditions within your market.

With this description of your target market characteristics, your company can clearly differentiate itself from competition. In addition, this information will allow your company to choose where to put marketing and sales resources. But there is still one more picture your company must bring clearly into focus. What obstacles may lie in the road ahead for your marketing and sales staff? To paint this picture, your company needs to know the distinctive capabilities of your competition. Your company needs a map that will allow your sales and marketing staff to take advantage of your company's service and product features and to avoid areas where your company can not compete well against your competition.

UNDERSTANDING YOUR COMPETITOR'S DISTINCTIVE CAPABILITIES

A description of your competitor's distinctive capabilities will make it clear where your company has advantages over the competition and where it may be at a disadvantage. It will tell your staff what your competition does, what your competition does well, what the industry's customers think of your competitors, how well your competition meets the requirements of the industry's customers, and how your competition's service performance has led to long-term customer relationships.

A clear description of your competitor's distinctive capabilities enables your company to choose the prospective customers that fit its distinctive capabilities better than your competitors'. With this complete picture of all three elements, you can maximize the process of growing your business. Your marketing and sales staff will have a customer-driven road map that will allow your company to take advantage of the shortest, most effective route to gaining new customers.

If your information has been customer-driven—incorporating information from customer surveys, industry experts, and feedback from your salesforce—you will have a picture of where your company stands. The process you are developing may point out deficiencies or changes in strategic directions you may need to address. But the purpose of this process is to maximize your marketing and sales process. What we will be focusing on is a step-by-step process that will minimize your company's sales costs by maximizing the return on your efforts. In other words, marketing and selling smarter.

FITTING YOUR DISTINCTIVE CAPABILITIES TO YOUR TARGET MARKET CHARACTERISTICS

The key ingredient in the Business Development Process is developing a two-way flow of information between your company and prospective customers. This flow of information begins by fitting together your company's distinctive capabilities with the characteristics of your company's target market. Ideally, this should be a perfect fit, where all aspects of your company's distinctive capabilities match your target market's characteristics. When services or products have been designed to meet the specific needs and service requirements of the target market, this should be the case.

If close investigation of the fit between the two reveals gaps or misfits, you will have to carefully consider the weaknesses this may present in increasing business. The alternatives to consider include altering your company's capabilities to fit the customer requirements of your company's target market, limiting the presentation of your company's capabilities to the target market so the misfit is not revealed, or adjusting the scope of who makes up your company's target market to better fit your company's distinctive capabilities.

Over time, the fit or misfit of all aspects of both your company's distinctive capabilities and your company's target market's needs and service requirements will change. This process of investigating fits and misfits should be regularly reviewed. Technology and economic factors will keep these dynamics in a constant state of flux. So a customer-driven company will constantly be looking to take advantage of change to keep their distinctive capabilities fitting the characteristics of their target market.

To illustrate this relationship between distinctive capabilities and needs and service requirements, let's look at an example. An exercise equipment manufacturer produces a variety of machines targeted to both the consumer market and exercise gyms. The exercise equipment manufacturer has worked hard to determine all the elements of the Business Development Process. The staff began by conducting surveys of their customers, interviewing their salesforce, conducting focus groups with both wholesalers and retailers, and collecting reviews from trade publications of equipment they produce as well as equipment produced by their competitors.

Their equipment has been designed to be as compact as possible, while offering a variety of exercises for both the upper and lower body. The equipment is highly flexible to adjust to different body sizes and shapes. Controls have been developed to allow for a wide range of experience levels, from the novice who just wants to stay in condition to the expert who is concerned with body building. Many options are available that are interchangeable with other products in the line. Every model is equipped with digital feedback monitors that allow the user to track heart rate, calories burned, and time spent, and to record recommendations for other exercises and recent workout performances. The equipment is priced at the mid-to-upper end of the market, but the modular features allow budget-conscious users to start with a small investment and add on as their needs and budget permit. The exercise equipment manufacturer puts a high priority on research and development of new products and improvements to old products.

Distinctive Capabilities

The exercise equipment manufacturer's distinctive capabilities can be described as a demonstrated ability to:

➲ Produce exercise equipment that features biofeedback displays.

➲ Provide the latest features in a compact and modular unit.

➲ Provide units that can be expanded and upgraded.

➲ Provide equipment that is guaranteed free from defect and that will maintain itself for the life of the product.

➲ Produce improved modular units with the latest technical advances that can be added to existing units, to meet the customer's needs into the future.

Target Market Characteristics

The exercise equipment manufacturer's target market characteristics can be described as follows:

➲ Customers show a desire for products with features that provides constant biofeedback to the user.

➲ Customers are generally very feature-sensitive, with some concern that they can purchase an entry level product in a price-sensitive market.

➲ Competition is mainly cost related, and limited because no other manufacturer produces a unit that can be expanded and upgraded in the future.

➲ Customers will pay more for equipment that is compact, modular, and of higher quality.

➲ There is a growing market of both consumer and exercise gyms that is trying to keep up with the latest technology.

Figure 3–1 illustrates the exercise equipment manufacturer's distinctive capabilities.

Figure 3–2 illustrates how the exercise equipment manufacturer's distinctive capabilities fit or fail to fit with the characteristics of the target market. The exercise equipment manufacturing company can use this illustration to pinpoint any misfits. If misfits exist, the equipment manufacturer may choose to modify the product to better fit the target market characteristics. If the manufacturer discovers, for instance, that the target market says customers' needs and service requirements include portability as a major characteristic, it may decide to buy lighter components and add wheels. Or it may decide to promote the stability and longevity of a stationary unit. While promoting stability and longevity might be a good strategy, it is not a customer-driven approach and may actually make it harder for the marketing and sales staff to promote the product.

The exercise equipment manufacturer investigation has revealed a good fit:

➲ The customers want information on their exercise performance.

➲ The product displays biofeedback information.

➲ Customers are sensitive to the features that are offered in making a buying decision.

➲ The equipment takes advantage of the latest features in a compact and modular unit.

Figure 3–1   Distinctive Capabilities

Exercise Equipment Manufacturer

Distinctive
Capabilities?

Produce exercise equipment that features biofeedback displays.

Provide the latest features in a compact and modular unit.

Provide units that can be expanded and upgraded.

Provide equipment that is guaranteed to be defect free for the life of the product.

Provide improved modular units with the lates technical advances that can be added to existing units, to meet future need.

FIGURE 3–2 THE FIT BETWEEN TARGET MARKET'S CHARACTERISTICS AND DISTINCTIVE CAPABILITIES

Exercise Equipment Manufacturer

Distinctive
Capabilities

Target Market
Characteristics

Distinctive Capabilities	Target Market Characteristics
Produce exercise equipment that features biofeedback displays.	Customers show a desire for products that provide constant biofeedback to user performance.
Provide the latest features in a compact and modular unit.	Customers want the latest features and are feature-sensitive.
Provide units that can be expanded and upgraded.	Customers want a unit that fits their budget now, and can expand with future upgrades.
Provide equipment that is guaranteed to be defect free for the life of the product.	Customers will pay more for equipment that is compact, modular, and of higher quality.
Produce improved modular units with the latest technical advances that can be added to existing units, to meet future customer need.	Customers demand the latest technical advances that can be updated to their units.

- ⊃ The target market wants a unit that will fit their budget now, and that they will be able to upgrade in the future.
- ⊃ The units are designed to be expandable and upgradable.

- ⊃ Consumers will pay more for equipment that will last.
- ⊃ The manufacturer stands behind the product with a guarantee that the product will remain free from defect for the life of the product.

- ⊃ The target market is growing and demands the latest technical advances.
- ⊃ There is a growing market for the product that can be upgraded with technical advances through open architecture design.

This illustration will become the model for the two-way education process designed to turn prospects into long-term customers. This is the foundation for growing your company's business. But if we stop here, the model will not be complete. If your company were the only one providing the service or product you offer, marketing and sales would be easy. Unfortunately, this situation rarely exists; and if it does, it won't exist for long.

How Your Competitors' Distinctive Capabilities Fit/Fail to Fit Your Target Market Characteristics

All providers of services and products have competitors. We need to construct a model of the fit or misfit that exists between our target market and our competitors' distinctive capabilities. This model will help your staff understand where your company may be unable to gain market share and where it will face a greater challenge in conducting a two-way education process. The model will also point out where your staff can use your company's advantages to fit the target market characteristics better than the competition can.

Let's first look at the distinctive capabilities for the exercise equipment manufacturer's competition. The competitor also manufactures a range of exercise equipment targeted to both the consumer market and to exercise gyms. Its equipment offers a variety of exercises for both the upper and lower body. The equipment is adjustable to different body sizes and shapes. A range of controls allows for a wide range of experience levels, from the novice to the expert. Models are equipped with digital feedback monitors, so users can track heart rate, calories burned, and time spent, as well as record recent workout performances. The equipment is priced at the mid-to-upper end of the market and is built in the same heavy-duty fashion as professional gym equipment; however, not all the features are included on the consumer model. The competitor manufacturer researches the latest developments in new products and adapts those features to its machines.

COMPETITOR'S DISTINCTIVE CAPABILITIES

The competitor's distinctive capabilities are a demonstrated ability to:

➲ Produce exercise equipment that includes biofeedback features.

➲ Provide the latest features in exercise equipment.

➲ Provide units that are large and stable and that work well.

➲ Provide equipment guaranteed free from defect and able to maintain itself for the life of the product.

➲ Produce equipment that meets the minimum needs of the consumer without all the features of professional gym equipment.

Using this description, we need to examine how the distinctive capabilities of the exercise equipment manufacturer's competition fit or fail to fit the characteristics of their target market.

Figure 3–3 is a model of how the competitor's distinctive capabilities fit/fail to fit the target market characteristics:

➲ The customers want information on their exercise performance.

Exercise Equipment Manufacturer

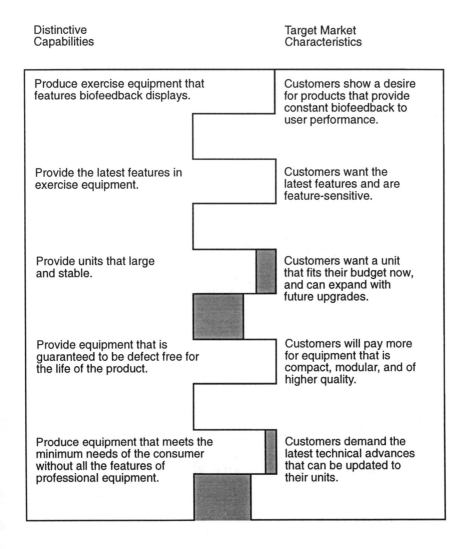

Distinctive Capabilities	Target Market Characteristics
Produce exercise equipment that features biofeedback displays.	Customers show a desire for products that provide constant biofeedback to user performance.
Provide the latest features in exercise equipment.	Customers want the latest features and are feature-sensitive.
Provide units that large and stable.	Customers want a unit that fits their budget now, and can expand with future upgrades.
Provide equipment that is guaranteed to be defect free for the life of the product.	Customers will pay more for equipment that is compact, modular, and of higher quality.
Produce equipment that meets the minimum needs of the consumer without all the features of professional equipment.	Customers demand the latest technical advances that can be updated to their units.

⮩ The product displays biofeedback information.

This is the same good fit as our manufacturer.

⮩ Customers are sensitive to the features that are offered in making a buying decision.

⮩ The equipment takes advantage of the latest features.

This is also a good fit.

⮩ The target market wants a unit that will fit their budget now, and that they will be able to upgrade in the future.

⮩ The units are stable and well built.

This is clearly a misfit; the competitor cannot meet the customer requirement for a modular unit that can be upgraded in the future.

⮩ Consumers will pay more for equipment that will last.

⮩ The manufacturer stands behind the product with a guarantee that the equipment will remain free from defect for the life of the product.

This is an exact fit of the customer's requirement.

⮩ Customers will pay more for equipment that is compact, modular, and of higher quality.

⮩ The consumer model is a stripped-down version of the exercise gym model.

This is not a good a fit, since it can be assumed that the exercise gym version has all the latest features and is of higher quality, and the consumer will not see all the same features on their home model, and it will be of a lesser quality.

Summary

Your target market is defined by how well your company's distinctive capabilities fit or fail to fit the characteristics of your target market. A customer-driven approach permits your company to understand your company's distinctive capabilities in terms of what matters most to your target market. Knowing how those distinctive capabilities meet the requirements shared by companies in your customer's industry will identify where fit exists or fails to exist. With this foundation in place you will now be able to build the Business Development Process and grow your company's business.

4

Distinctive Capabilities

Distinctive capabilities are those abilities that set your company apart from the competition. In this section, you will learn how to lay the foundation for future business development success. By analyzing the five aspects of your company's distinctive capabilities, you will later be able to clearly and succinctly educate prospective customers.

Your company's objective is to describe the five aspects that make up its distinctive capabilities: service or product definition, major service or product distinction, established reputation, quality service focus, and customer service distinction.

Description of Service or Product

The first aspect of your distinctive capabilities is your company's proven ability to provide its service or product. You need to describe, in a precise manner, the customer-driven reason your company is in business. When communicated internally and externally, this description will help drive success in increasing sales revenue.

Your description can be as brief as one sentence, or it can consist of several sentences. In either case, it should be the key definition of what your company does. This should be well understood by marketing and sales staff as well as the company's staff at large.

EXAMPLE

> *Software Company A produces a software package that enables doctors to integrate appointments, billing, and bookkeeping. The customer-driven description for Software Company A's product is shown in Figure 4–1.*

DESCRIPTION OF MAJOR SERVICE OR PRODUCT DISTINCTION

The second aspect of your company's distinctive capabilities is its proven ability to distinguish its service or product from the competition. Again, this should be a precise description of the customer-driven reason your service or product is distinct from the competition. Why should a prospective customer choose your service or product over the service or product of a competitor?

In developing this description, you should take into consideration information from several different sources. Talk to members of the development team and review information used in their original development of your company's service or product. Interview your salesforce and consider what is being presented to prospective customers in sales presentations. Ask customer service personnel to relate customer comments and their experiences in working with customers. Also have your marketing department review relevant information gathered from customer surveys.

EXAMPLE

> *To continue with our example of Software Company A, we need to develop a description of the company's major service or product distinctions. From information gathered during the creation of the product, an easy-to-understand user interface was identified as an important feature to the customer. When interviewed, the salesforce felt the product's features were easier to sell to specialized practices as opposed to a general practice. Customer surveys revealed that the time savings by office staff was the most significant feature distinguishing the product from other office automation products.*

Figure 4–1   Description of Major Service or Product Distinction

Distinctive Capabilities

I. Description of service or product:

The proven ability to automate scheduling, billing, and patient record keeping and integrate medical record keeping, insurance claims, and the administration of medical services with financial management requirement of a family clinic environment.

II. Description of major service or product distinction:

_____
_____
_____

III. Description of established reputation:

_____
_____
_____

IV. Description of quality service focus:

_____
_____
_____

V. Description of customer service distinction:

_____
_____
_____

> *All of these features could describe the distinctions of the software product. And all should be considered in the final statement. But in weighing the sources of information, remember that we want to be sure that the description is customer-driven.*
>
> *The customer-driven description of Software Company A's product distinction is shown in Figure 4–2.*

Description of Established Reputation

The third aspect of your distinctive capabilities is the current reputation your company has established. This description can be more difficult to define. An established reputation is a distinctive capability your company has built with customers over time. Reputation by definition is a customer-driven characteristic. The positive perception that has been built in your customer's mind can be shared with prospective customers, giving your company the distinction of an established reputation in the target market.

Your description may be derived from testimonials, provided by customers who have reordered your service or product time and again. The least biased source is reviews or articles in trade publications. Industry experts may contribute to the production of these articles, and third-party endorsements build reputations more quickly and with greater significance.

Example

> *In the case of Software Company A, its reputation may have been established by earlier products or earlier versions of this particular software product. Within the industry, it may have established a reputation as a leader in constructing innovative user interfaces, with a proven understanding of the day-to-day workings of a specialized medical clinic. Such an established reputation will carry significant weight with prospective customers.*
>
> *Software Company A's description of its established reputation is shown in Figure 4–3.*

Figure 4–2   Major Service/Product Distinction

Distinctive Capabilities

I. Description of service or product:

The proven ability to automate scheduling, billing, and patient record keeping and integrate medical record keeping, insurance claims, and the administration of medical services with financial management requirement of a family clinic environment.

II. Description of major service or product distinction:

The proven ability to develop unique user interface, saving staff time in the scheduling, billing, and patient record keeping of specialized medical functions.

III. Description of established reputation:

IV. Description of quality service focus:

V. Description of customer service distinction:

Figure 4–3   Established Reputation

Distinctive Capabilities

I. Description of service or product:

The proven ability to automate scheduling, billing, and patient record keeping and integrate medical record keeping, insurance claims, and the administration of medical services with financial management requirement of a family clinic environment.

II. Description of major service or product distinction:

The proven ability to develop unique user interface, saving staff time in the scheduling, billing, and patient record keeping of specialized medical functions.

III. Description of established reputation:

The proven ability to comprehend customers' situations, and provide solutions to everyday administration needs of a medical facility, in a time effective manner.

IV. Description of quality service focus:

V. Description of customer service distinction:

Description of Quality Service Focus

The fourth aspect of your company's distinctive capabilities is your staff's proven ability to focus on quality service. In describing quality service focus, you must define "quality service" as the ability to meet the needs and requirements of your customers. Quality service is not just doing a good job. In our customer-driven approach to defining distinctive capabilities, quality service is meeting your customers' needs and service requirements.

Many of the resources for obtaining information discussed earlier in this chapter will also be used in developing this aspect of your distinctive capabilities. In particular, customer surveys obtained through written questionnaires, from phone interviews, or better still from in-person visits to customers will provide the information necessary to establish your customers' needs and service requirements. Review the steps your company presently takes to meet the needs and service requirements of current customers. Are these steps taken to meet the customer's needs or your company's? If your company's definition of quality service is responding to service calls within an hour, and your customer's definition of quality service is never having a service call, your definition is not customer-driven.

Example

Software Company A has spent a good deal of time listening to customers. From these interviews it has established that its customer expectations are met when a product can be brought into the clinical environment and implemented with a minimal amount of downtime. Customers expect to achieve a measurable result in efficiency as soon as the product is up and running.

Software Company A's quality service focus is shown in Figure 4–4.

Description of Customer Service Distinction

The fifth aspect of your distinctive capabilities is your company's proven ability to develop a customer service distinction, which differs

FIGURE 4–4   QUALITY SERVICE FOCUS

Distinctive Capabilities

I. Description of service or product:

The proven ability to automate scheduling, billing, and patient record keeping and integrate medical record keeping, insurance claims, and the administration of medical services with financial management requirement of a family clinic environment.

II. Description of major service or product distinction:

The proven ability to develop unique user interface, saving staff time in the scheduling, billing, and patient record keeping of specialized medical functions.

III. Description of established reputation:

The proven ability to comprehend customers' situations, and provide solutions to everyday administration needs of a medical facility, in a time effective manner.

IV. Description of quality service focus:

The proven ability to meet customers' expectations of ease of installation, operation, and immediate and significant gains in efficiency.

V. Description of customer service distinction:

from established reputation and quality service focus. Here you will want to define your company's long-term commitment to customers.

A long-term commitment in a customer-driven definition of distinctive capabilities must be thought of in win-win terms. For the customer, this distinction means a constant commitment by your company to meet the customer's changing needs. For your company, this customer service distinction must mean a long-term profitable relationship.

Your description should take into account information used in your company's strategic planning because this type of distinction characterizes the type of long-term customer your company is built around. Over time relationships with long-term customers will be the most valuable to your company. Reviewing the history of these customers will reveal significant information about marketing, sales, operations, customer service, and profit potentials.

Example

> Software Company A's customer service distinction may have come from a history of major accounts. These accounts all have several common characteristics. First, they all have been users of either earlier versions of the product or other types of products developed by Software Company A.
>
> What has kept these customers over the long term? What has made them fit into a successful profit model? In this case, customer-driven research revealed that the software producer's ability to constantly out-anticipate the user's needs by reengineering the product has kept loyalty high. Software Company A has developed a profit model based upon customers who will want software upgrades. This type of customer is profitable because they are willing to pay the high price charged for product upgrades.
>
> Software Company A's description of its customer service distinction is shown in Figure 4–5.

By bringing together information that clearly defines the five aspects of your company's distinctive capabilities, you will be able to define the customer-driven reasons your company operates as a business. You can now succinctly focus on what your company contributes to the customer; what differentiates your service or product from competitors; what perceived reputation your company's performance

FIGURE 4–5   CUSTOMER SERVICE DISTINCTION

Distinctive Capabilities

I. Description of service or product:

The proven ability to automate scheduling, billing, and patient record keeping and integrate medical record keeping, insurance claims, and the administration of medical services with financial management requirement of a family clinic environment.

II. Description of major service or product distinct:

The proven ability to develop unique user interface, saving staff time in the scheduling, billing, and patient record keeping of specialized medical functions.

III. Description of established reputation:

The proven ability to comprehend customers' situations, and provide solutions to everyday administration needs of a medical facility, in a time effective manner.

IV. Description of quality service focus:

The proven ability to meet customers' expectations of ease of installation, operation, and immediate and significant gains in efficiency.

V. Description of customer service distinction:

The proven ability to maintain profitable long-term relationships by continuous customer-driven improvements to products.

has established; how well your company understands and meets the needs and service requirements of your customers; and how your company has produced long-term, mutually beneficial relationships with customers.

Summary

To summarize your company's distinctive capabilities, review the sample distinctive capabilities worksheets for Software Company A. On the following page is a blank worksheet (worksheet A) you can reproduce to summarize your company's distinctive capabilities. As we proceed through the Business Development Process, you will use this summary of distinctive capabilities to fit into your company's model of the target market's characteristics. The resulting match will become the foundation for growing your business.

Chapter 4

WORKSHEET A—DEVELOPING DISTINCTIVE CAPABILITIES

Distinctive Capabilities

I. Description of service or product:

_____
_____
_____
_____

II. Description of major service or product distinction:

_____
_____
_____

III. Description of established reputation:

_____
_____
_____

IV. Description of quality service focus:

_____
_____
_____

V. Description of customer service distinction:

_____
_____
_____

TARGET MARKET CHARACTERISTICS

Target market characteristics are common needs and requirements shared by companies in a particular industry. For instance, a group of companies in a particular industry may share common needs and service requirements for the target market of an information services provider. They require electronic data interchange between suppliers and customers, sharing of a large database that must be updated quickly, remote network access, on-line message system to link them with suppliers and customers, and security access privileges. It is important to define the scope of a particular industry to produce common requirements. The more diverse the industry, the less common the requirements.

This chapter will help you determine your company's target market characteristics. By understanding a common set of needs and requirements, your staff will be able to better understand the individual needs of prospective customers.

Your objective is now to describe your company's target market characteristics. These five common characteristics are: compatibility, cost-buying factor, geographic characteristics, competition in the target market, and market factors.

EXAMPLE

> *For an example of target market characteristics, we will look at a different industry than the software producer. In this chapter, we will use the example of Printing Company B. But before we define the printing company's target market capabilities, we need to become familiar with their distinctive capabilities.*
>
> *Printing Company B has conducted research on external and internal customers. From this information, they have summarized their distinctive capabilities in a customer-driven description. Printing Company B provides high-quality, multiple-color printing, with both web (continuous form fed) and sheet-fed presses. An example of its work might include a full-color, 24-page brochure with large color photos, printed on high-gloss paper. Its customers tend to be larger corporations who print product brochures in large quantities. Printing Company B has chosen to bring in-house many of the peripheral outside services it relies on in producing printed matter. By no longer depending on outside vendors for color separations, bindery, die-cutting, and so on, Printing Company B has been able to decrease production time, control output quality, increase communication, and control costs. Printing Company B has built its reputation on bringing its customers the best quality printing available and producing it on time. Its customers have identified proactive communication as the major reason that problem situations are rectified before they derail a job. When problems have occurred, Printing Company B has taken the initiative and made things right at its own expense. This has given it the reputation of standing behind their work.*
>
> *Printing Company B has defined its distinctive capabilities in Figure 5–1.*

DESCRIPTION OF COMPATIBILITY

As with your description of distinctive capabilities, this description must be precise. When you look at your customers and prospective customers in a particular industry or area, do your distinctive capabilities remain constant with the service needs and product requirements of the target market? This is the test for compatibility. A statement of how well your company's distinctive capabilities remain constant with customers in the target market will become your description of compatibility. A clear understanding of the flexibility of your distinctive

FIGURE 5–1   DISTINCTIVE CAPABILITIES WORKSHEET

Distinctive Capabilities

I. Description of service or product:

Established ability to provide high-end, color printing.

II. Description of major service or product distinction:

Established ability to turn around complex jobs with a variety of sophisticated
in-house equipment.

III. Description of established reputation:

Established ability to produce error-free work, on-time.

IV. Description of quality service focus:

Established ability to provide printed materials to meet the exact requirements
of the customers.

V. Description of customer service distinction:

Established ability to maintain profitable long-term customers by combining
outstanding customer service with high standards for quality.

capabilities, and an honest assessment of where they do not match, will define your market as well as determine where you should and should not spend resources.

EXAMPLE

> With the stage set for our printing company, let's take a closer look at the first requirement of target market characteristic. The description of compatibility for the printing company is shown in Figure 5–2.

DESCRIPTION OF COST-BUYING FACTOR

The second target market characteristic is your customer's cost-buying factor. Cost-buying factor can be defined as the value your customer places on the different criteria that go into making a purchasing decision. In business all too often, the saying goes, "You can have speed, quality, and price. Pick any two." This is not a customer-driven statement. In today's business environment, customers may very well want all three. However, the statement is a generalization, and most customers will place varying degrees of value on speed, quality, and price. The cost-buying factor tries to define where and in what proportion the target market places value.

EXAMPLE

> Printing Company B's target market places a higher value on speed over cost. Customers in the target market are willing to pay a higher price in order to receive printed material as quickly as possible. Secondly, the target market places less value on cost than on quality. Customers within the target market will pay a premium for the highest possible quality. Lastly, the target market places equal value on speed and quality. The target market's customers do not want to sacrifice either quick turnaround time or the best possible job in printing its projects. Its description of their its market's cost-buying factor is shown in Figure 5–3.

FIGURE 5-2   DESCRIPTION of COMPATIBILITY

Target Market Characteristics

I. Description of compatibility:

Customers' needs for high-end color printing produced on-time with proactive communication, match with the company's ability to provide that service.

II. Description of cost-buying factor:

III. Description of geographic characteristics:

IV. Description of competition in the target market:

V. Description of market factors:

Chapter 5

FIGURE 5-3   DESCRIPTION OF COST-BUYING FACTOR

Target Market Characteristics

I. Description of compatibility:

Customers' needs for high-end color printing produced on-time with proactive communication, match with the company's ability to provide that service.

II. Description of cost-buying factor:

Customers are generally more service-sensitive than price-sensitive.

III. Description of geographic characteristics:

IV. Description of competition in the target market:

V. Description of market factors:

Description of Geographic Characteristics

The third target market characteristic is used to define the needs and requirements placed on your company's market due to geography. Is the scope of your operations defined by location? Are the supply channels affected by location? Is there a geographic network for distribution? All of these factors will contribute to your description of the geographic characteristics that make up your target market.

You will need to begin by defining the scope of your target market. If your company's customers are located in local or regional areas, your description will be limited to this scope. Your company's customers may be distributed over a larger area, multiple regions, the entire domestic market, or even worldwide. Whatever the case, different geographic areas may define different customer requirements that make up your target market. If these requirements are different from one another, you will need to develop a separate group of target market characteristics for each differentiated market. Each market will have different resources, different regulations, and different competitive forces that will affect both the target market characteristics and your company's distinctive capabilities. In addition, if this is the case, you should also review your distinctive capabilities to see if they should be different depending on market.

Example

> *Printing Company B is located on the West Coast. Their headquarters and plant are located in Portland, Oregon. Sales offices are located in Seattle, Portland, San Francisco, and Los Angeles. Each sales office has an established customer base in each location. Their description of geographic characteristics is shown in Figure 5–4.*

Description of Competition in the Target Market

The fourth description of the target market defines what advantages your company has over competitors.

Competitor information can come from a variety of sources. If your company's competitors are publicly held, annual reports are an

FIGURE 5–4   DESCRIPTION of GEOGRAPHIC CHARACTERISTICS

Target Market Characteristics

I. Description of compatibility:

Customers' needs for high-end color printing produced on-time with proactive communication, match with the company's ability to provide that service.

II. Description of cost-buying factor:

Customers are generally more service-sensitive than price-sensitive.

III. Description of geographic characteristics:

The market is focused on major corporate headquarters located on the West Coast, with sales, production, and distribution channels well defined.

IV. Description of competition in the target market:

V. Description of market factors:

excellent source of information. Trade publications are another good source. Your salesforce can also provide you with information from common customers or with information gathered in competitive sales situations. Customer surveys also provide information about customers' perceptions of the competition.

Your description of competition in your target market should include the factors that limit your competitors from taking away market share. What requirements do your customers have that limit competitors' ability to take those customers away? For example, Printing Company B may have a press that allows it to print large format posters, while competitors do not have that large a printing press, and the cost for them to obtain such a press is prohibitive. Another issue to consider is your competitors' location or distribution channels. Do your competitors' locations allow them to provide the target market with an advantage? Is there a pricing or service advantage?

By answering these questions, you will be able to draw a clear picture of your competition. This information needs to be clearly communicated to all marketing and sales personnel. In the next chapter, we will go into a deeper analysis of competitors' distinctive capabilities.

Example

> To return to our example of Printing Company B, let's look at its description of competition in the target market. Printing Company B has advantages over competitors on the West Coast because of several factors.
>
> First, only a few competitors have both a large web (continuous form fed) and sheet-fed, large format printing press, and only a few printers have kept pace with the technology Printing Company B has brought in-house. Examples include advanced color separation equipment with digital imaging and manipulation functions, and advanced computer controlled digital image-to-plate-to-press.
>
> Second, competitors have chosen to locate their printing plants in major cities, where all of their customers are based. Consequently, the competitors have to focus on only one major city or to construct printing production facilities in multiple locations. Printing Company B has chosen a single plant site in Portland, Oregon, but can easily serve the same customer base through an effective transportation, communication, and sales network.

Third, competitors have chosen to locate their salesforce in their main printing plant in a single core city. Printing Company B's sales staff is strategically positioned. Sales offices have been located in major geographic territories, where they are in close proximity to the headquarters of major corporations. Competitors' sales staffs are generally made up of employees who have risen through the ranks of various printing functions and have now become salespersons. Printing Company B emphasizes training for its sales staff, and has selected sales staff both for their knowledge of printing, and their understanding of the processes and requirements facing the corporation's corporate communication departments. In addition, the printing company continuously trains its staff in new technologies and challenges that face corporate communication.

Last, competitors have much longer sales cycle because of the delays in manually determining estimates, alteration charges, delivery dates, and project status. Printing Company B has used technology to facilitate proactive communication. By using state-of-the-art scheduling software, customers can be kept up-to-date on the progress of their job. Sales offices at remote locations can tie into the company's computer to have immediate knowledge of potential problems that may cause delays.

By clearly reviewing each of the areas where competitors might challenge them, the printing company defines its competition in the target market as shown in Figure 5–5.

Description of Market Factors

The final target market characteristic you will need to describe is the overall factors that affect your market. Examples of these market factors might include the general economy, the economic health of industries that make up your target market, profitability characteristics for your service or product, and new competitive challenges that may conflict with your advantages.

Your analysis should take into account information used in regular reviews of your company's strategic plan. It is critical to thoroughly research all of the conditions that make up the overall factors that affect your target market. Sources for this information include local economic forecasts, national economic forecasts, trade publications for your company's industry and trade publications for your company's target market, your staff's own analysis of costs factors in producing

FIGURE 5–5   **DESCRIPTION OF COMPETITION IN TARGET MARKET**

Target Market Characteristics

I. Description of compatibility:

Customers' needs for high-end color printing produced on-time with proactive communication, match with the company's ability to provide that service.

II. Description of cost-buying factor:

Customers are generally more service-sensitive than price-sensitive.

III. Description of geographic characteristics:

The market is focused on major corporate headquarters located on the West Coast, with sales, production, and distribution channels well defined.

IV. Description of competition in the target market:

Competition is limited due to large format presses and in-house equipment capabilities, customer needs for high-end printing, quick communication, project deadline requirements, and sales staff's close proximity to customer locations.

V. Description of market factors:

your company's service or product, your own analysis of pricing factors affecting your company's service or product, and information obtained from your salesforce and from customers.

EXAMPLE

> *Printing Company B needs to regularly monitor the overall market factors of their target market. The effects of the economy on the target market, of costs from suppliers, of new technology, and of increased capability from competitors are constantly changing.*
>
> *A no-growth or slow-growth economy means that the companies that make up their target market are going to be extremely cautious with pricing. It is extremely important to justify any increased cost with either service or product benefit, or Printing Company B will have to refine internal processes to keep costs competitive. Current pricing is profitable; however, there is concern that availability of paper from suppliers may have an effect. Also, the cost of new technology that may be required to keep ahead of new competitors may affect long-term overhead costs. A careful eye needs to be kept on the competition. Do they have plans to expand? What new equipment or technology is planned that would pose a challenge? Are competitors making advances toward any of the sales staff? Printing Company B's description of overall factors of its target market is shown in Figure 5–6.*

SUMMARY

Describing its target market characteristics allows your company to clearly define the requirements the target market has for your company's service or product; the balance that exists between price and quality of service or product in your target market; the effect of the location of your company's prospective customers and your distribution location on your company's target market; the characteristics that make up your company's competition in the target market; and the effect that the economy, production costs, and competitive challenges place on your company's target market.

To summarize your company's target market characteristics, review the sample target market characteristic worksheet for Printing Company B. On page 54 is a blank worksheet (worksheet B) that

FIGURE 5–6 DESCRIPTION OF MARKET FACTORS

Target Market Characteristics

I. Description of compatibility:

Customers' needs for high-end color printing produced on-time with proactive communication, match with the company's ability to provide that service.

II. Description of cost-buying factor:

Customers are generally more service-sensitive than price-sensitive.

III. Description of geographic characteristics:

The market is focused on major corporate headquarters located on the West Coast, with sales, production, and distribution channels well defined.

IV. Description of competition in the target market:

Competition is limited due to large format presses and in-house equipment capabilities, customer needs for high-end printing, quick communication, project deadline requirements, and sales staff's close proximity to customer locations.

V. Description of market factors:

A large market with consistently profitable characteristics, continually changing economic, and competitive factors that must be constantly monitored.

Worksheet B—Developing Target Market Characteristics

Target Market Characteristics

I. Description of compatibility:

_____
_____
_____
_____

II. Description of cost-buying factor:

_____
_____
_____

III. Description of geographic characteristics:

_____
_____
_____

IV. Description of competition in the target market:

_____
_____
_____

V. Description of market factors:

_____
_____
_____

you can use to summarize your company's own target market characteristics. With a clear description of the common requirements shared by companies making up your target market, you will be able to match your company's distinctive capabilities with your description of your target market's characteristics. The match between distinctive capabilities and target market characteristics make up two of the three elements that will build the cornerstone for the Business Development Process. The more you understand these elements, the better you will be at using the Business Development Process to grow your company's business.

Competitor's Distinctive Capabilities

A competitor's distinctive capabilities are the abilities of your competition to meet the requirements of your company's target market. With a clear understanding of your company's competitor's distinctive capabilities, you will be able to position your company to better fulfill the requirements of your target market.

In the previous chapter, we developed a description of competitions in the target market. Now your staff will need to produce a more in-depth definition of the distinctive capabilities of your company's competitors. You will need to describe your competitor's service or product, major service or product distinction, established reputation, quality service focus, and customer service distinction.

Example

> To describe each of the aspects of the competitor's distinctive capabilities, we will use a business called Cellular Service Company C as an example. First we will review the distinctive capabilities and target market characteristics of Cellular Service Company C, then we will look at Cellular Service Company C's competitors' distinctive capabilities.
>
> Briefly, let's profile Cellular Service Company C. the company is one of two main providers of cellular air time networks. In addition, there are a handful of other resellers of cellular air time, who do not own their own network but buy bulk blocks of time and resell them to subscribers. Our Cellular Service Company C has the first digital network and has several

> service features that the competition has not yet matched. Its service area is defined by a major metropolitan city and several smaller adjacent cities and suburbs. Price, service package, and corporate discounts for group subscribers appear to be the major reasons that customers choose them over the competition.
>
> The distinctive capabilities of Cellular Service Company C are shown in Figure 6–1 and its target market characteristics are shown in Figure 6–2.

Description of Competitor's Service/Product

The first aspect of your competitor's distinctive capabilities you will need to define is their ability to provide their service or product. To determine your competitor's ability to provide its service or product, you will need to obtain competitor information. As mentioned in the last chapter, sources of competitor information may include annual reports (if the competitor is publicly held); trade publications; your salesforce, either from discussions with common customers or from sales staff who previously may have worked for competitors; and information gained from customer surveys. Once your staff has assembled this information, your company can develop an accurate description of the competitor's service or product.

Example

> Now let's take a look at the distinctive capabilities of Cellular Service Company C's competitor. As already mentioned, there is only one main competitor providing a cellular network in this region. There are a handful of resellers of bulk cellular time, but the research our cellular service provider has conducted with customers and prospective customers has revealed that they are not identified as a major alternative to provide service. The major reason for this is that the resellers lack the capital and marketing resources to create enough awareness of their capabilities.
>
> The main competitor, however, has been identified as equally attractive for providing a cellular network and service to prospective customers. It offers a very competitive rate but it includes a limited number of features. It does not yet have a digital network, nor does it offer as many services. Its service area covers the same region; however, within the region are areas where its network has difficulty providing quality service. It does not offer a discount

FIGURE 6-1   DISTINCTIVE CAPABILITIES WORKSHEET EXAMPLE

Distinctive Capabilities

I. Description of service or product:

Substantiated ability to supply air time, with full featured cellular phone service, over a broad network.

II. Description of major service or product distinction:

Substantiated ability to provide cost competitive service, with a wide variety of customer specified features including call forwarding and voice mail.

III. Description of established reputation:

Substantiated ability to provide the latest available features, without service failures.

IV. Description of quality service focus:

Substantiated ability to provide cellular phone service to meet the exact requirements of customers including 24-hour customer service, automated credit for dfopped calls, and loaner phones when a phone needs repair.

V. Description of customer service distinction:

Substantiated ability to maintain profitable long-term customers by providing competitive rates and 24-hour customer service.

**FIGURE 6–2   TARGET MARKET CHARACTERISTICS WORKSHEET
                 EXAMPLE**

Target Market Characteristics

I. Description of compatibility:

Customers require a full range of services beyond just air time, which is
consistant with the features provided.

II. Description of cost buying factor:

Customers are generally very price-sensitive, with a secondary concern that
service requirements are met.

III. Description of goeographic characteristics:

The market is well defined by the regional service area coverage of the network
and limited due to the technical ability of current equipment.

IV. Description of competition in the target market:

Competition is limited to one other major supplier who is limited in ability to
provide customer requirements due to equipment that is less technically
advanced.

V. Description of market factors:

Growing concentration of users in a defined region, with continued pressure
for more service features provided at a reduced price.

package to corporate group customers. Its current policies do not provide the same ease of customer service. Users will find it much more difficult to get credit for interrupted calls. Surveys have revealed however, that some prospective customers would rather have fewer services for a more competitive price.

The description of the competitor's distinctive capabilities is shown in Figure 6–3.

Description of Competitor's Major Service or Product Distinction

In developing a description of your competitor's major service or product distinction, it should be pointed out that what you are attempting to establish is a point of distinction. What distinguishes your competitor's service or product from your company's service or product ? This may be a distinction in service or product that is advantageous to your company in a customer-driven perspective, or it may be to your company's disadvantage. For example, the competitor does not have the same service area as Cellular Service Provider C, giving a distinction that is advantageous to Cellular Service Provider C. The only other alternative is that there is no distinction in service or product between your company and the competitors. If that is the case, your company will be locked into a constant battle over price. Your company's ability to grow your business will be limited without some sort of feature differentiation.

Establishing a point of distinction needs to be as unbiased as possible. It is not always easy to be unbiased about a point of distinction that may or may not be to your advantage. For this reason, information sources that are most preferable are customer and prospective customer surveys, and information gained from trade publications. Another possible source may be advertisements or promotional material from the competition. However, be sure your staff is able to distinguish between a competitor's actual service or product capabilities and the claims the competitor is making.

Figure 6-3   Description of Competitor's Service or Product

Competitor's Distinctive Capabilities

I. Description of competitor's service or product:

Provides service to the same area, with fewer services at a competitive rate.

_____

_____

_____

II. Description of competitor's major service or product distinction:

_____

_____

_____

III. Description of competitor's established reputation:

_____

_____

_____

IV. Description of competitor's quality service focus:

_____

_____

_____

V. Description of competitor's customer service distinction:

_____

_____

_____

Example

> Cellular Service Company C's competition's distinction of service will be a disadvantage to the competition. It has spot areas its network cannot consistently reach. In addition, it does not offer group discount plans for corporate subscribers and have limited customer service, and it is difficult for customers to obtain credit for service interruptions. The description of competitor's major service or product distinction is shown in Figure 6–4.

Description of Competitor's Established Reputation

As in describing your own established reputation, you need to define your competitor's established reputation that has been built up over time. The single best source of this type of information is your own salesforce. Often in sales situations, one of the roadblocks that salespeople must overcome is the established reputation of the competition. Other sources that may be useful include customer and prospect surveys, and articles in trade publications that refer to your company's competitors.

Example

> Cellular Service Company C's competitor has a reputation for lower prices but incomplete network and limited services. The description of its competitor's reputation characteristic is shown in Figure 6–5.

Description of Competitor's Quality Service Focus

It is worth repeating that we are defining quality service focus as determining the customer's needs and service requirements first, and then using your company's capabilities to meet these requirements. The essential purpose of this process is to maintain a customer-driven approach. That is, be sure you are defining your customer's needs and service requirements in their terms not yours.

FIGURE 6–4   DESCRIPTION of COMPETITOR'S MAJOR SERVICE OR PRODUCT DISTINCTION

Competitor's Distinctive Capabilities

I. Description of competitor's service or product:

Provides service to the same area, with fewer services at a competitive rate.

_____

II. Description of competitor's major service or product distinction:

Limited service area with few customer service programs.

_____

III. Description of competitor's established reputation:

_____

IV. Description of competitor's quality service focus:

_____

V. Description of competitor's customer service distinction:

_____

Figure 6–5   Description of Competitor's Established Reputation

Competitor's Distinctive Capabilities

I. Description of competitor's service or product:

Provides service to the same area, with fewer services at a competitive rate.

II. Description of competitor's major service or product distinction:

Limited service area with few customer service programs.

III. Description of competitor's established reputation:

Low cost, with limited service.

IV. Description of competitor's quality service focus:

V. Description of competitor's customer service distinction:

Earlier, when you determined your company's quality service focus, you went through a process of determining your customer's needs and service requirements. Your staff may have conducted customer surveys through written questionnaires, phone interviews, or in-person customer visits. By analyzing this information, your company has come to a clear understanding of what your customers want from your service or product. This process will not change here. Only the steps taken by the competitor to identify the perspective customer's needs and service requirements, and the competitor's efforts put into meeting those needs and requirements will vary. This variance will differentiate your company from the competition. If your staff is able to establish that your competitor manufactures a product that performs slower than your company's product, and performance was identified as a need or service requirement by the customer, then this is how your competitor's quality service is differentiated from your company's.

Example

> Cellular Service Company C, through surveys they have conducted and with research performed by an independent consultant, has determined that the competitor is meeting the customers' needs when it comes to low cost. But the research also shows that it is unable to meet the exact customer service requirement to deliver a complete network of service 100 percent of the time. In pinpointing the target market, this has become a clear point of distinction. The description of the competitor's quality service focus is shown in Figure 6–6.

DESCRIPTION OF COMPETITOR'S CUSTOMER SERVICE DISTINCTION

The last point of distinction between your company and your competition is your competitor's proven ability to develop a customer service distinction. As mentioned when we discussed your company's distinctive capabilities, customer service distinction differs from established

Figure 6–6   Description of Competitor's Quality Service Focus

Competitor's Distinctive Capabilities

I. Description of competitor's service or product:

Provides service to the same area, with fewer services at a competitive rate.

_____

_____

_____

II. Description of competitor's major service or product distinction:

Limited service area with few customer service programs.

_____

_____

III. Description of competitor's established reputation:

Low cost, with limited service.

_____

_____

IV. Description of competitor's quality service focus:

The proven ability to meet the price requirements specific to customer needs.

_____

_____

V. Description of competitor's customer service distinction:

_____

_____

_____

reputation and quality service focus. What we want to determine is your competitor's long-term commitment to customers.

In some industries more than in others, it is much more difficult to gain this type of information. For most companies, the salesforce will be the best source of this information. If you were to ask members of your sales staff for the reasons they are not able to take business away from competitors, their answers may reveal the customer service distinctions of your competition. Customers stay with their current provider of service or product because they see a mutually beneficial relationship.

Other sources of this type of information include articles in trade publications profiling competitors. Customer surveys can also be a source of this type of information; however, the best information will come from your customers who formerly used the competition. Independently administered studies by a consulting group of your industry, particularly if they are produced on a regional or local basis, are a very effective means of gaining this type of insight into your competitor's customer service distinction.

How your staff gathers the information will depend on the size of your organization, the marketplace, and the availability of the information. Be sure not to overlook your own salesforce. If they are regularly face-to-face with new prospects, they are more than likely all too familiar with the competition's customer service distinction.

EXAMPLE

> *Cellular Service Company C's sales staff has related many instances where prospective accounts were lost because the competitor's ability to maintain a relationship with the prospective customer was based on keeping its costs low. Even though these prospective customers were willing to give up service and innovative features, Cellular Service Company C has retained a distinct part of the market. This is evident in its own description of customer service distinction.*
>
> *The description of customer service distinction for Cellular Service Company C's competitor is shown in Figure 6–7.*

By describing your competitor's distinctive capabilities, your company will be able to get a clear picture of how your competitor's

Figure 6–7 **Description of Competitor's Customer Service Distinction**

Competitor's Distinctive Capabilities

I. Description of competitor's service or product:

Provides service to the same area, with fewer services at a competitive rate.

II. Description of competitor's major service or product distinction:

Limited service area with few customer service programs.

III. Description of competitor's established reputation:

Low cost, with limited service.

IV. Description of competitor's quality service focus:

The proven ability to meet the price requirements specific to customer needs.

V. Description of competitor's customer service distinction:

The proven ability to maintain profitable long-term relationships by being the price leader.

fit with the characteristics of your company's target market. Your staff will now be able to summarize the following:

- ➲ What services and products your company's competition offers prospective customers.

- ➲ What distinguishes the competitor's service or product.

- ➲ What reputation the competition has established in the target market.

- ➲ How well the competition meets the needs and service requirements of prospective customers in the target market.

- ➲ What points of distinction make your competitor's customers loyal to them over time.

SUMMARY

In summarizing your company's competitor's distinctive capabilities, review the sample competitor's distinctive capabilities worksheets for Cellular Service Company C throughout this chapter. On the following page is a blank worksheet (worksheet C) that you can use to summarize your company's competitor's distinctive capabilities. With a clearly defined description of the competition's distinctive capabilities, your staff's next task will be to determine where your competitor's distinctive capabilities fit and do not fit the characteristics of your company's target market. This fit or lack of fit between distinctive capabilities and target market characteristics make up the foundation of the Business Development Process. Your staff should now take the time to illustrate your own company's fit/misfit model. Use worksheet C to develop your company's competitor's distinctive capabilities. Use worksheet D to develop a fit/misfit model for your company's distinctive capabilities and target market characteristic. Use worksheet E to develop a fit/misfit model for competitor's distinctive capabilities and target market characteristic. By understanding your company's distinctive capabilities, your company's target market characteristics, and the distinctive capabilities of your competitors, your staff can build the dynamics of a marketing and sales process that will maximize the use of your company's resources.

Worksheet C—Developing Competitor's Distinctive Capabilities

Competitor's Distinctive Capabilities

I. Description of competitor's service or product:

_____
_____
_____
_____

II. Description of competitor's major service or product distinction:

_____
_____
_____

III. Description of competitor's established reputation:

_____
_____
_____

IV. Description of competitor's quality service focus:

_____
_____
_____

V. Description of competitor's customer service distinction:

_____
_____
_____

Fit/Misfit Model

Distinctive
Capabilities

(Indicate fit or misfit
for each aspect
of the model.)

Target Market
Characteristics

I. _____

Fit: _____

I. _____

Misfit: _____

II. _____

Fit: _____

II. _____

Misfit: _____

III. _____

Fit: _____

III. _____

Misfit: _____

IV. _____

Fit: _____

IV. _____

Misfit: _____

V. _____

Fit: _____

V. _____

Misfit: _____

Worksheet E—Developing a Fit/Misfit Model for Competitor's Distinctive Capabilities and Target Market Characteristics

Fit/Misfit Model

Competitor's Distinctive Capabilities	(Indicate fit or misfit for each aspect of the model.)	Target Market Characteristics

I. _____
_____
_____

Fit: _____

Misfit: _____

I. _____
_____
_____

II. _____
_____
_____

Fit: _____

Misfit: _____

II. _____
_____
_____

III. _____
_____
_____

Fit: _____

Misfit: _____

III. _____
_____
_____

IV. _____
_____
_____

Fit: _____

Misfit: _____

IV. _____
_____
_____

V. _____
_____
_____

Fit: _____

Misfit: _____

V. _____
_____
_____

PART II

THE ELEMENTS
AND BENEFITS

Integrating Marketing and Sales Functions

In Part I, we identified the elements of the Business Development Process model and developed an understanding of how it works as well as how distinctive capabilities, target market characteristics, and competitor's distinctive capabilities fit or fail to fit. In Part II, we will build an understanding of the different marketing and sales functions that will be necessary. Once we understand the basic elements and benefits of integrated marketing and sales, we will focus on the tools that will be utilized to create two-way education during the thirteen-steps that form the Business Development Process.

Integrated Marketing

Marketing and sales have become increasingly more sophisticated over the last twenty years. Companies large and small can no longer depend on the conventional salesforce, whether one person or a large national sales network, to be the source of growing a business. Neither can companies depend on several independent sources to generate business. A multimethod plan, which approaches different audiences in different fashions, can no longer guarantee success. Prospective customers have become much more savvy to having their needs understood and met.

In the past, it was a sellers' market. Prospective customers would buy general solutions to specific problems because there were few service or product providers who would spend the time developing solutions to specific problems. An environment existed where there were a lot more customers than suppliers. A printer might set the amount of time needed to produce a brochure, even if the customer wanted it sooner. A manufacturer would set specific features that customers had to choose from, rather than asking customers what features they wanted.

This environment has changed fundamentally. Now, it is a buyers' market. The business environment has evolved into an extremely competitive marketplace. Prospective customers can now demand that their specific needs and service requirements be met by a supplier. If the supplier does not conform, there are other suppliers who will gladly step in. In today's environment a printer is much more likely to adapt its schedule to meet the customer's timeline, rather than lose the customer to a competitor.

In such a competitive buyers' market, suppliers of services and products will naturally find it more challenging to get their message across to the target market. In addition, the message is much more complex than before. In the past, a generalized message—We do everything well!—could be used. The printer would sell on the basis of all kinds of printing from one-color forms to full-color brochures. And a generalized message is much easier to communicate from one or several independent sources. The printer, for example, could send salespeople to knock on doors at office parks and get enough business. Now, the message must not only be specific—We do *this* well—it must also be prefaced with the question—What are your needs? The printer now specializes in high-quality annual reports, because its customers have said that is what their needs are. To accomplish this, a supplier must have a strategic approach that brings together different means of communication. It is fundamental that two-way communication be established, with each marketing and sales activity planned to accomplish a specific objective of the communication process. And most importantly, those marketing and sales resources must be integrated to maximize efficiency while determining and meeting the specific prospective customer's needs and service requirements. The printer now must use a combination of advertising, telemarketing, direct mail, and a salesforce to meet its sales revenue goals.

An integrated approach, combining your marketing and sales resources, will greatly improve the probability of sales for two important reasons. First, prospective customers can gain deeper understanding of your service or product when the message is constructed over time rather than all at once. Second, prospective customers can make their needs known as this integrated approach progresses. Figure 7–1 illustrates the power of this integration of marketing and sales resources.

Because your use of integrated marketing and sales resources will more quickly educate your company to the requirements of your company's target market, and your company's prospective customer will be educated more quickly to your company's distinctive capabilities, your company will need fewer prospects to generate sales. The end result will be more "fits" of specific prospective customers to your company, and thus an increase in the growth of your business. The Business Development Process will show you the process that will strategically use these different forms of marketing and sales resources in an integrated fashion.

Advertising

Advertising has always been used as a shotgun approach to broadcasting capabilities to a potential market. In the Business Development Process, instead of a shotgun approach, advertising can be used for two purposes. First, it can be strategically used to raise the level of awareness of a target market. Second, it can be used as an interactive way to build preliminary interest and give the target market a vehicle to respond with their needs and service requirements. Advertising in this respect is not looked at as a means to gain sales, but as a vehicle that can inform and educate.

Figure 7–1 Probability of Sales Versus Number of Sales Contacts Using an Integrated Marketing Approach

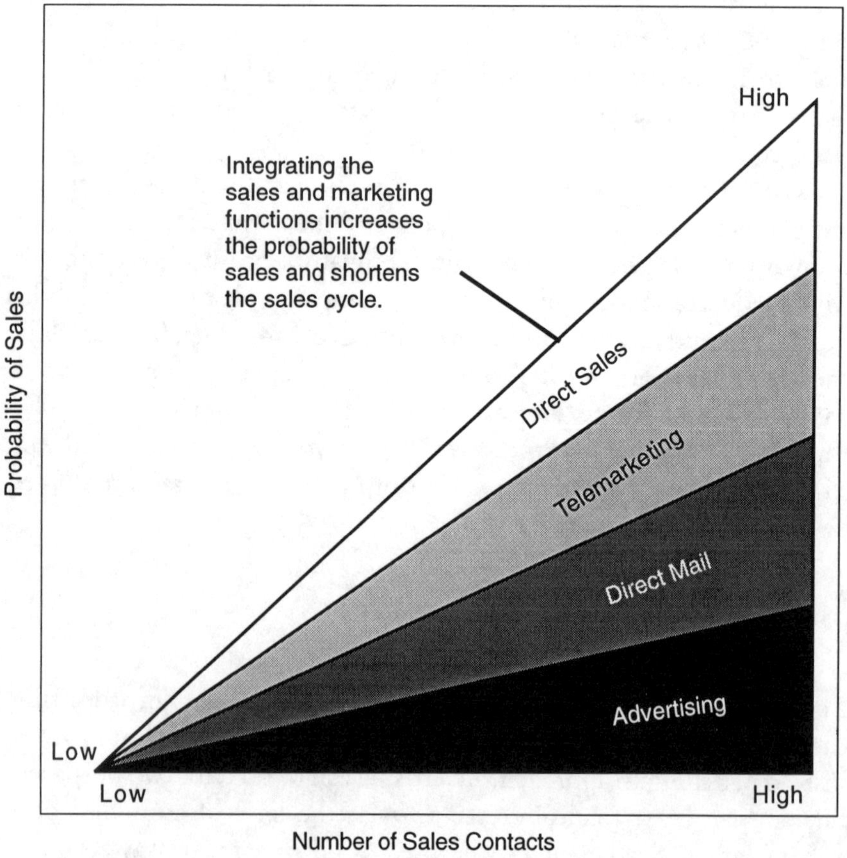
Integrating the sales and marketing functions increases the probability of sales and shortens the sales cycle.
High
Low
Direct Sales
Telemarketing
Direct Mail
Advertising
Low
High
Probability of Sales
Number of Sales Contacts

Telemarketing

Traditionally, telemarketing has been used to quickly present a company's service or product capability, make an offer, and ask for a commitment. In the Business Development Process, telemarketing is used only to gain information from the target market. Telemarketing is considered a means to find out who the primary decision maker is and, more importantly, to construct a preliminary model of the prospective customer's needs and service requirements.

Direct Mail

Direct mail has dramatically increased in sophistication over the past decade. In many cases, direct mail is used to present a company's capabilities, to make an offer, and to obtain a commitment. In the Business Development Process, direct mail is used in several ways. But again, the Business Development Process uses direct mail to inform the target market of your company's capabilities, and in an interactive manner to gain information from the target market about their needs and service requirements.

Direct Sales

Direct sales through a salesforce has been relied on as the major source of informing a target market as well as securing sales. Typically, a direct salesforce has had to generate cold calls, qualify the lead, develop a relationship, produce and present the proposal, and finally ask for the business. In the Business Development Process, the salesforce is looked upon as having the closest associations and understanding of the target market. Therefore, it is the role of direct sales to build a much deeper relationship between the company and the prospective customer. The salesforce is looked on as the experts at developing a valuable benefit that is readily apparent to the prospective customer. The valuable benefit is a direct result of the fit between your company's distinctive capabilities and their needs and service requirements.

In the next chapter, we will discuss the resources you will need to put the Business Development Process model into action for your company. In Part III, you will begin to develop a detailed understanding of how to begin applying these resources to the Business Development Process.

8

Knowing Your Resources

In this chapter, we will discuss some of the people, management, and informational resources necessary to implement the Business Development Process. Utilizing communication tools effectively, having personnel who will create informational tools and contact prospects, having data in an easily accessible and manipulative format, and keeping it all working together are critical to the success of the Business Development Process. There are any number of ways to implement this process. This chapter illustrates some possible ways to implement the process.

To begin, let's take a closer look at the bull's-eye target introduced in Figure 2–1. This illustrates the Business Development Process model divided into four concentric rings. The four rings represent stages of the process, made up of a series of thirteen steps. Each ring has a different function within the model, requiring the use of communication tools.

Preliminary Qualification—The Outer Ring

The steps in the outer ring begin qualifying a group within the selected target market. Selection of this group is determined by setting criteria for the prospective customers that have the greatest likelihood of becoming long-term customers. You may determine that your company has a better success rate with medium-size companies, so those will be your first targets.

Once you have determined a target prospect group, they will need to be qualified. The Business Development Process will establish several methods for qualifying prospects. Phone or written surveys are one method that will provide qualification information determining the decision maker, qualification characteristics, and so on.

Another approach might be through programs that allow the target prospect group to qualify itself. Advertising in a manner that gives the prospective customer an 800 phone number or a reader service card to express interest is one method. Another might be to develop a direct mail/direct response mailing, where the prospect can return a postage-paid card expressing interest. Trade shows represent an environment where prospects can qualify themselves simply by coming to an exhibit and entering a lead-generation contest. Seminars and presentations that invite prospective customers to gain particular knowledge offer an alternative means for prospective customers to qualify themselves.

Figure 8–1 illustrates the preliminary qualification steps that make up the outer ring.

Preliminary Qualification Tools

Letters A variety of letters, customized to fit individual prospective customers' needs and service requirements, need to be written. These will take the form of introductory letters, a series of information letters that may be accompanied by other materials, or letters that ask for specific customer requirements. Additional follow-up letters and thank-you notes also may be necessary. You may wish to build a library of standard letters that can be customized to fit specific needs and prospective customers. Planning and testing these letters at the beginning of this process will be a big time saver as you move prospects through the Business Development Process. As we will discuss a little later in this chapter, you may want to integrate these letters into a sales lead/tracking software product to further automate your process.

Brochures An introductory brochure may be used as part of the Introduction step. (See description in outer-middle ring.)

Phone Telemarketing is one form of communication that is integrated into the Business Development Process. Personnel are necessary

FIGURE 8–1   PRELIMINARY QUALIFICATION—THE OUTER RING

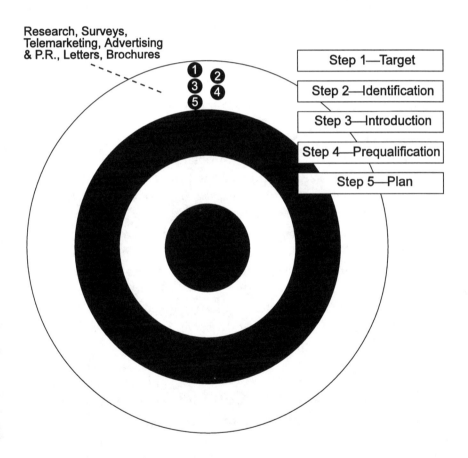

Research, Surveys, Telemarketing, Advertising & P.R., Letters, Brochures

Step 1—Target

Step 2—Identification

Step 3—Introduction

Step 4—Prequalification

Step 5—Plan

to complete actions that require phone skills. These individuals have to feel comfortable with their phone skills, as well as be effective in communicating or obtaining the information objectives of the call.

During the Business Development Process, telemarketing will be used in prospective customer identification, prospective customer qualification, surveying prospective customer qualifications, and confirmation of prospective customer's receptiveness.

Surveys To obtain information about prospective customers, you will need to develop several types of surveys. These may include written surveys that are mailed to the prospective customer, scripts for phone surveys, and questionnaires that are completed in face-to-face interviews. During the Business Development Process, individual surveys will have different objectives. Initial phone interviews may qualify the prospective customer. Other interviews during this exchange of information may determine the prospective customer's needs and service requirements.

Surveys need to be crafted to obtain the desired information. Care needs to be taken not to lead the prospect to a predetermined conclusion. The survey design must be open-ended enough to give prospective customers the ability to express their individual perceptions, but specific enough to obtain your objectives. The form the survey takes will also dictate its length and the type of information that can be determined. Again, it is more effective to build a collection of different types of surveys that you can customize for different prospect customers and different target markets. It is important to remember that the production of a survey is not as easy as it may appear and can be a time-consuming process.

MARKETING AND SALES COMMUNICATION PROCESS— THE OUTER-MIDDLE RING

The steps in the outer-middle ring provide an exchange of information. This may be done primarily by using direct mail in different forms. Sales presentations may serve a similar function.

As this exchange of information is two-way, prospective customer interviews to determine requirements will be needed. Each of the four steps that make up this stage will require increasingly more sophisticated approaches to inform prospective customers of distinctive capabilities and to extract their needs and service requirements. These steps are illustrated in Figure 8–2.

MARKETING AND SALES COMMUNICATION PROCESS TOOLS

Direct Mail/Response When carefully crafted, direct mail/response can be one of the single most effective tools in identifying prospective customers whose needs and service requirements fit your company's distinctive capabilities. In the Business Development Process, direct mail/response can take any number of forms. The most effective are those that can succinctly communicate an offer with enough value to the prospective customer that they will return the communication.

A direct mail/response piece can make several kinds of offers. The objective of the offer is to motivate prospective customers to confirm their interest in your service or product. By qualifying themselves, the prospect is responding that there is a fit between their needs and service requirements and your company's distinctive capabilities. In addition, the response should identify details of the prospect's specific needs and service requirements, or obtain specific information regarding a prospective customer's priorities in making a buying decision.

Brochures Brochures are one of the major vehicles to communicate your company's distinctive capabilities. A series of brochures will be necessary for both direct mail and presentations. Some of these brochures will be informational, and some will try to gain a specific response from the prospective customer. Brochures will range in message from those that present a simple view of your company's service or product to those that go into detail about the customer-driven benefits of your company's distinctive capabilities.

The number of brochures necessary for companies to communicate with their target market will vary greatly. The presentation of your service or product will depend on the services or products your company offers, the size of your company, and the complexity of the target market.

Service/Product Sheets A service/product sheet is a one-page information sheet that summarizes facts about a specific service or product.

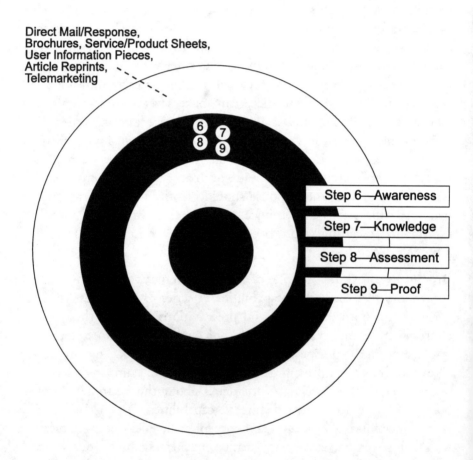

Direct Mail/Response,
Brochures, Service/Product Sheets,
User Information Pieces,
Article Reprints,
Telemarketing

Step 6—Awareness

Step 7—Knowledge

Step 8—Assessment

Step 9—Proof

This type of communication piece is particularly useful in conveying one aspect of a company's distinctive capability. In addition, it is also very useful in overcoming a specific objection from a prospective customer by clearly communicating the fit to a prospective customer's need or service requirement. Printing Company B for example, might produce an $8^1/2$ x 11 product sheet that includes a color photo showing printed samples of posters, product brochures, and annual reports. Below the photo bulleted text lists features that are distinctive capabilities and benefits that meets the customer's corresponding need or service requirements.

Over time, we are trying to build a fit with prospective customers as we move them to the center of the target. One-page service/product sheets offer a means to accomplish this without cluttering the message. A library of one-page service/product sheets can be a cost-effective way to pinpoint specific advantages of your company's distinctive capabilities that fit the prospect's needs and service requirements.

User-Information Pieces As a prospective customer reaches the middle-inner ring of the target, you will need to begin to offer proof of the claims you have been making to educate the prospective customer about your company's distinctive capabilities. User-information pieces consist of detailed material that gives specifics as to how your company's service or product is used.

The distinction between user-information pieces and brochures should be clear. Brochures communicate your company's distinctive capabilities and can also be a means for requesting information from the prospective customer. In a brochure, your company describes all of the services or products that your company offers to customers. It is a vehicle for your company to tell what a great job your company does in delivering the distinctive capabilities. User-information pieces demonstrate to the prospective customer how your company's service or product can be put into operation by the prospective customer. The user-information piece gives prospective customers useful information that they can apply directly to meeting their needs or service requirements. An example the printing company might use would be a customer guide to producing an annual report. This would include a step-by-step planner, a calendar for establishing a schedule, and a formula for specifying cost estimates.

Article Reprints When offering prospective customers proof of your distinctive capabilities, article reprints are an effective means of communicating a third-party endorsement. In addition, your staff may use articles that are not specifically about your company but that offer specific information about how the type of service or product you offer is important to the target market.

For example, the printer might send an article on how effective printing a direct mailer was for a similar type of company that is interested in expanding their business.

A library of relevant articles needs to be collected over time. It is important to keep this library of articles current and to discard articles that may become out of date.

Phone Telemarketing may be used as part of the Assessment step. (See description in outer ring resources.)

Marketing and Sales Development Team— The Inner-Middle Ring

The inner-middle ring is where the actual package of service or product to be presented to the prospective customer is designed. The proposed service or product package will need to fit the prospective customer's exact needs and service requirements with the company's distinctive capabilities.

The team of marketing and sales development needs to bring together all the information that has been exchanged through the earlier steps of the process and develop a strategy to meet the prospective customer's need. In addition, operational staff, customer service representatives, and product developers need to be brought into the equation, along with pricing information.

The next function of this step is to present the strategy in the form of a solution that is in the prospective customer's language and understandable from their perspective. This is a customer-driven approach. The proposal needs to be prepared by your marketing and sales development team, whose members have an intimate knowledge of the prospective customer's needs and service requirements. All of the groundwork that has been done earlier in the process will be wasted if the marketing and sales development team does not skillfully advance the process at this step. All questions and concerns about the fit between the prospective customer's needs and service requirements and your company's capabilities must be thoroughly answered. If this has been done, a customer-driven process will yield a service or product that adds benefits for the prospective customer. Figure 8–3 illustrates these steps.

Marketing and Sales Development Team Tools

Strategy Teams Key marketing and sales staff need to be involved in strategy sessions that precede the development of a tailored proposal. Depending on the particular solution that is being developed to meet the prospective customer's needs and service requirements, the strategy team will expand to include other staff members. These staff members may come from a range of functions including: research and development, operations, customer service, administration, and management.

Proposals To make distinctive capabilities known, to demonstrate an understanding of the needs and service requirements of the prospective customers, and to present a solution, you will need to have personnel who are skilled at communicating the written word, as well as illustrating graphic messages.

Sales Management—The Center Ring

The steps in the center ring culminate the sale and turn a new customer into a long-term customer. This stage requires sales management. For our purpose, we will define sales management as your company's monitoring of the customer's implementation of the service or product, and investigating future opportunities to expand your business.

To create long-term customers, monitoring processes must be in place that can identify any potential gaps in service or product performance. Your staff must have the ability to turn any potential misfit into a fit. In other words, you must watch for any potential problems that may arise and have a system in place to fix them. This practice

Figure 8–3   Marketing and Sales Development Team—
The Inner-Middle Ring

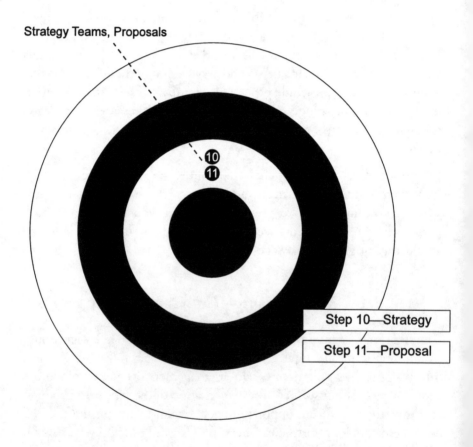

Strategy Teams, Proposals

Step 10—Strategy

Step 11—Proposal

will lead to long-term profitable customers who consider their relationship with your company a "win-win" situation. Figure 8–4 illustrates the final two steps.

Sales Management Tools

Salesforce In a conventional sales system, sales staff may be responsible for cold calling, qualifying, creating a proposal, and closing the sale. In the Business Development Process, prior to the sales staff's involvement, the targeted prospect group has been selected, prospective customers have already been qualified, and a two-way exchange of information has taken place. When the sales staff does become involved, there is a high probability of a close fit between your company's distinctive capabilities and the prospect's needs and service requirements.

The Business Development Process strategically integrates each element of the marketing and sales process to maximize its effectiveness. Doing this saves the sales staff for what it does best. In the latter stages of the process, the objective of the sales staff is to present proof of the fit between the two companies, work with the marketing staff to develop a strategy, present the proposal, gain approval for the sale, and build a long-term relationship with the prospect.

RESOURCES NECESSARY TO IMPLEMENT THE BUSINESS DEVELOPMENT PROCESS

Utilizing resources effectively is another part of marketing and selling smart. Your company may already have many of these resources in one form or another. Necessary resources for the Business Development Process include: communication pieces, personnel tasks, a salesperson network, database management, and management systems. Investments in these resources will bring your company financial returns if the resources contribute to the management or exchange of information.

Figure 8–4   Sales Management—The Center Ring

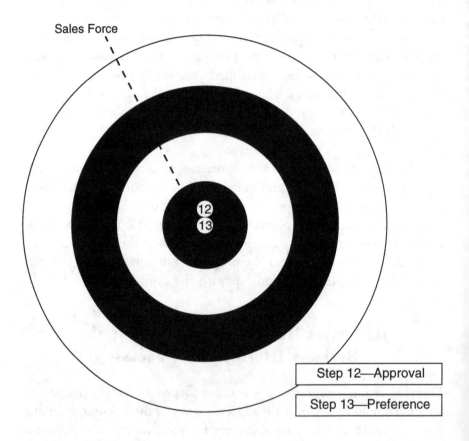

Sales Management
The Center Ring

Communication Pieces

To accomplish an effective two-way exchange of information, you will need to create communication pieces that educate your target market about your company's distinctive capabilities and communication pieces that give prospective customers the ability to communicate their needs and service requirements to your company. A communication piece may serve one or both functions, but in both cases, the objective is to use information to match distinctive capabilities with the target market's characteristics.

Personnel Tasks

The most important ingredient in the Business Development Process is the staff that will be responsible for implementing the process. The marketing and sales staff that are assigned the tasks of implementing the process will need to initiate, coordinate, track, and maintain the flow of prospects from the outer edge of the bull's-eye target model to its center. In a small business, these responsibilities may all be assigned to one person; in a larger company, a staff of five or more may be needed. Before the Business Development Process is initiated, be sure your staff has a clear understanding of the requirements of each process.

Salesperson Network

Your company's salesforce, whether it is made up of one person or a large network of salespeople, is critical to the success of the Business Development Process. The salesforce needs to be integrated into the process. The skills and expertise that your sales staff brings to the process will strengthen the strategies and facilitate closing the sale. As a prospect moves to the inner two rings of the target model, your company's sales staff becomes involved. By integrating sales and marketing functions, the Business Development Process uses direct marketing technique to move the prospective customer through the outer rings, and the salesforce to bring the prospective customer to the center by developing specific solutions to customer's needs and closing the sale. When you consider the high cost of salespeople making cold calls, this is a wise savings in the use of your marketing and sales dollars.

DATABASE MANAGEMENT

The Business Development Process will generate enough information to be tracked that a database will be necessary to maintain it. A small company with limited sales resources and a small target market, and a large company with multiple target markets will both need an automated system to keep the process on track and recall information when necessary.

MANAGEMENT SYSTEM

This chapter points out the need for overall system management of the Business Development Process. Who will be the prospective customers that make up the current target prospect group? What communication pieces exist to communicate your company's distinctive capabilities? Whose responsibility will it be to determine the prospective customers' needs and service requirements? At what point should the prospective customer's receptiveness be measured? Who should be part of the team that develops the strategy for the proposal? Who presents the proposal and gains acceptance of your company as a vendor? And who measures the extent to which the customer's needs and service requirements are being met? A monitoring and management system will need to be in place up front for all of these issues to be handled as part of the overall process.

Prospect Tracking As multiple prospective customers or multiple target prospect groups progress through the Business Development Process, they need to be carefully tracked. Not every prospective customer will make it to the center of the bull's-eye target. Some will not qualify and will be misfits rather than fits. Others will progress at different rates through the process.

Each prospective customer has specific strategies developed to match distinctive capabilities with its needs and service requirements. Marketing and sales resources will need to be coordinated in order to demonstrate the match between the prospective customer and your company.

Writing During the two-way education process, some communication pieces will need to be customized. Proposals, letters, and requests for specific proof of the fit that may exist between your company and the prospects are all examples of pieces that will require writing skills of your staff. Your company may want to use a staff member with excellent writing skills or a freelance writer to set up generic letters of introduction, letters that accompany direct mailings, and generic proposals, all of which can later be modified by your marketing or sales staff who are experts in your particular service or product.

Mailing The use of direct mail/response has already been discussed as an integrated approach in the Business Development Process. A major ingredient in any direct mail/response effort includes a well-managed mailing program. This also involves the careful coordination and tracking of prospects. Keep in mind, a major element of failure can be incorrectly mailed or mistimed mailings.

Communication Integrating the different marketing and sales elements of the Business Development Process takes coordination and, most importantly, communication. The more prospective customers your company has going through the bull's-eye target model—each moving at their own rate, each with different strategies to create a fit, each requiring the use of different marketing and sales resources—the greater the need for clear communication between all those involved.

Your company's sales staff needs to be able to anticipate the number of prospective customers that will be targeted. The amount will probably be dictated by the size of your marketing and sales staff. When prospective customers reach the inner-middle ring, sales must be part of the two-way education process, so they do not enter into the process cold. Conversely, the marketing staff will need to be kept informed as part of the strategy process.

Defining Turf The conclusion we can draw from this discussion of communication is that your company's marketing and members of the sales staff need to know their roles and work together as a team, even if your staff consists of only two or three members. An integrated approach demands that each member of your company's marketing and sales staff know his or her areas of responsibility, know the requirements of those responsibilities, and be aware of how his or her role fits into the overall process. An entire marketing and sales team must take responsibility for communicating progress with one another throughout the Business Development Process.

Databases A database will need to record what companies make up your target prospect group, along with names addresses, and so on. As the process progresses, you will need to record more detailed information about the prospective customer. A calendar will also need to be kept in the database for planned communications, and to keep a record of what was sent to a particular prospective customer and the customer's reaction. The more detailed information you enter into your database about a particular prospective customer, the more customized the output you can create in automated production of communications material. When contacting multiple prospective customers at the same stage of the Business Development Process, databases and word-processing programs can perform mail merges to greatly speed up the process.

Depending on your company's resources, your staff can develop a simple solution to recording prospective customer information and tracking. This information could be kept in a series of forms. However, given the features of standard database software and word processors, the time savings would easily justify spending the time and money to set up an automated solution.

Several sophisticated software packages exist for contact management. This type of software integrates word processing; a database; and calendar programs including reminder alarms, electronic rolodex, customer report generation, auto dialing/modem interface, and note taking, all combined into one easy-to-use package with a simplified user-interface.

ACT! by Symantec, is one such program. It combines all the features listed above, plus many more. The most impressive part of the program is how you can customize many of its features, formats for prospect records, and forms for letters and management reports to fit your company's needs. Detailed prospect information can be stored in ACT!'s records, and prospective customers can be grouped by any number of parameters. Everything from letters to proposals can be stored in ACT!, modified for a particular prospective customer or for a group of prospects. The program will remind you of scheduled communications with prospects. In addition, ACT! will make notes of any information your staff records and produce reports that detail the latest information on prospective customers. This is just one of several such programs that can save your staff a great deal of time and make it more effective.

The same system will also provide your marketing and sales staff with reports. Such reports can be customized to meet internal communication needs. This type of report can be used to keep all members of your staff aware of current prospective customers moving through the Business Development Process.

Tracking We have already discussed the use of a database to keep track of prospective customers; now we will consider the type of information that will need to be tracked. As your company's target prospect group advances through the bull's-eye target model, each prospective customer's progress will need to be managed. Your marketing and sales staff will need to designate a member of your team to be responsible for managing the movement of prospective customers. This individual will need to use whatever data management system your company chooses to keep track of all members of the prospect group.

Depending on the size of your company, the individual(s) that manages the tracking, communication, and scheduling may be the same staff member(s). In a larger organization, a small core team of staff may manage all these tasks. In some cases, different internal teams may be set up to manage different target prospect groups throughout the process. This may be especially effective in regional applications if your salesforce is spread out over a large geographic area. Or if your company offers different services or products, applying teams to manage the process based on the different service or product may be extremely effective. For example, Printing Company B might create a team to manage prospective customers in the Southern California market.

Management A small company that institutes this process will have to carefully maintain records. Even with a small marketing and sales staff or no marketing and sales staff at all, the progress of prospective customers through the process and the two-way flow of information will need to be coordinated.

A larger company, with a larger marketing staff at the home office and sales staff at satellite offices, will have proportionately greater needs. The larger company will need a larger target prospect group and a more diverse flow of information between the company and prospective customers as well as between the marketing and sales staff.

Internal Communications The Business Development Process manages the two-way flow of information between your company and the target market to maximize the efficiency of your marketing and sales efforts, resulting in the fit of your company's distinctive capabilities with the prospective customer's needs and service requirements. This communication process can easily break down if all members of your marketing and sales staff do not communicate the status of prospective customers. As with tracking, one individual should be assigned responsibility to manage internal communication of the process. This individual will need to keep all members of the marketing and sales staff up-to-date with the progress of individual prospective customers within the target group. Additionally, this team coordinator will need to make sure that all members of the marketing and sales staff understand their responsibilities. This job function includes coordinating tasks by different participants as well as anticipating resources to successfully move a prospective customer to the center of the bull's-eye target.

Scheduling Every prospect within your company's target prospect group will move through the process at a different rate. One individual will need to be responsible for maintaining a schedule for all prospective customers. This schedule will need to be maintained and communicated with all participants. As results of communications with the prospective customer are reported back to this individual, schedules and adjustments in strategy may need to be made.

Establishing Goals Goal setting should be part of your company's Business Development Process. The goal may be the number of target prospect group members that make it to the center ring of the target. An effective measure might be the amount of margin dollars the process generates. Especially early in the implementation process, a goal may be the quantity of prospective customers that have reached different stages of the bull's-eye target. Be prepared to adjust your goals while your company is new at the Business Development Process. As your marketing and sales staff gains experience with moving prospective customers through the process, they will be better able to set realistic goals.

Meeting Expectations As you have reviewed this section on knowing your company's tools and resources, you may have realized the amount of work that is necessary in implementing the Business Development Process. But by taking the time to strategically plan what target markets will bring your company the best possible chance of gaining new profitable business, your company can integrate marketing and sales functions to maximize sales and effectively use marketing and sales resources. The return of this type of investment can bring a healthy increase to the growth of your company's business. How quickly these gains are made depends on several factors. Different industries require different amounts of time within the sales cycle. The amount of time your company's marketing and sales staff can allocate to the process will also greatly affect the results. More than anything, a consistently applied, well-managed process will be the key to meeting expectations.

PART III

PROSPECTIVE CUSTOMER
SELECTION

Business Development Process Step 1: Target

In Parts I and II of this book, you became familiar with the Business Development Process and the bull's-eye target model. In this Part you will be introduced to the first five steps of the thirteen-step Business Development Process. You will learn the techniques of developing two-way education, beginning with identifying prospective customers within selected target markets. Your staff will bring prospective customers toward the center of the bull's-eye through an exchange of information that educates prospective customers about your company's distinctive capabilities, while your staff understands and conforms to their needs and service requirements. Our first objective is to determine what prospective customers will make up the target prospect group. The next objective is to obtain addresses and phone numbers for the headquarters of companies within the target markets.

In Part I of this book, you determined how your company's distinctive capabilities fit or failed to fit the characteristics of your target market. You also gained an understanding of how your competition's distinctive capabilities fit or failed to fit the target market's characteristics. With that foundation in place, you are ready to begin the first step of the Business Development Process.

OVERVIEW OF TARGET PROSPECT GROUP

With the understanding you have gained of how your company's services or products meet your target market's needs and service requirements, your challenge is to identify potential prospective customers within that target market. As you begin this part of the process, your staff should select from the target market a group of prospective customers with the greatest potential for a good fit.

To determine which companies should make up your target prospect group, take a look at the profitable customers who currently have a relationship with your company. This list will contain current customers within your target market, where there is a good fit between the customer's needs and service requirements and your company's services or products. To build a more detailed profile of these companies, your staff will need to identify significant data about each customer. This data will include industry type, number of employees, approximate revenue, geographic location, number of offices, title of the decision maker, and the specific buying patterns each customer has exhibited.

As you produce this profile, it may be helpful to use standard industry classification codes (SIC) to identify the specific industry group to which customers belong. If you are not already familiar with SIC coding, it is a commonly used system to define companies by industry. SIC codes begin with a two-digit number that identifies a broad industry group. As the number of digits increases, the industry grouping becomes more specific. Four-digit SICs will give you a more focused segment of an industry. For instance, 5941 is the SIC code for sporting goods stores. Eigh-digit SICs will create an even more defined industry group. 5941-0400 is a subgroup for sporting goods stores that specifically sell exercise equipment.

To create the actual profile of the target market, you now need to group your customers by the data you have identified. Organize your groupings in the following order:

1. Industry group (4–8 digit SIC)
2. Service or product usage
3. Profitability per unit and volume

4. Geographic location

5. Approximate revenue of customer

6. Number of employees

To illustrate what a target market profile might look like, let's use the example of Printing Company B that we looked at in Part I.

To review, Printing Company B's distinctive capabilities are as follows:

➲ Proven ability to provide high-end color printing.

➲ Proven ability to turnaround complex jobs with a variety of sophisticated in-house equipment.

➲ Proven ability to produce error-free work, on time.

➲ Proven ability to provide printed materials to meet the exact requirements of customers.

➲ Proven ability to maintain profitable long-term customers by combining outstanding customer service with high standards for quality.

Printing Company B's target market characteristics are as follows:

➲ Customer's needs for high-end color printing produced on time with proactive communication match with the company's ability to provide that service.

➲ The target market places a higher value on speed over cost, less value on cost than quality, and equal value on speed and quality.

➲ Printing Company B has used technology to facilitate proactive communication.

➲ Competition is limited due to equipment capabilities, customer requirements, and strategic locations.

➲ The effect of the economy on the target market includes: costs from suppliers, new technology, and increased capability from competitors.

To begin building their target market profile, Printing Company B developed a report that detailed their top customers of the preceding year. The criteria for being included in the report included volume of printing, revenue generated, margin dollars created, type of material printed, and frequency of printing projects.

From this data, the printing company ranked their most profitable customers. Top customers created the largest total margin dollars for the year. Since Printing Company B places a high value on long-term relationships with customers, a secondary consideration was volume and frequency of printing. Then, margin per job was considered. By analyzing all these criteria, the top 100 customers were ranked. Figure 9–1 is an example of Printing Company B's top 100 customer list. Next, Printing Company B characterized each company by the type of material printed, (annual reports, capabilities brochures, product catalogs, product posters, etc.); industry type, including four-digit SIC codes; customer size in employees; estimated revenue if available; and geographic location.

The top 100 customers were then grouped to look for similarities. The first grouping was customer by industry. The second grouping was by type of material printed for the customer. The third grouping looked at the most profitable customers by printed units (profit per brochure, per poster etc.). The fourth grouping evaluated by location. The fifth grouping was established by estimated customer revenue as a company. The final grouping was done by the number of staff the customer employed. Figure 9–2 illustrates these groupings.

By cross tabulating and comparing each grouping, several interesting profiles began to emerge. The first was that the top twenty percent of the most profitable customers printed an annual report and at least one other major project per year. These projects all had a high profit per unit, and a long-term relationship existed with the customer. The second profile established that three main industry groups—computer and electronic companies, medical equipment companies, and manufacturers of consumer products—accounted for over 50 percent of the profit from the top 100 customers. The third profile found that geographic breakdown of the top 100 customers was spread out over the major metropolitan centers on the West Coast. The number of employees per customer and the customer-generated revenue corresponded directly to the overall profit per customer created from the material printed. Figure 9–3 shows the printing

FIGURE 9-1 PRINTING COMPANY B: TOP 100 CUSTOMERS

Ranking Most Profitable

Customer	Total margin	Units	Frequency	Margin per job
ABC Company	$650,000	500,000	5 per year	$130,000
DEF Company	$610,000	850,000	10 per year	$ 61,000
GHI Company	$550,000	200,000	2 per year	$275,000
JKL Company	$420,000	600,000	7 per year	$ 60,000
MNO Company	$375,000	150,000	3 per year	$125,000

Figure 9-2 Printing Company B: Top 100 Customers Groupings

Grouping By Industries

Customer	Industry	Items	Margin/unit	Location
GHI Company	High-tech	A. Report	$2.75	L.A.
MNO Company	High-tech	A. Report	$2.50	Seattle
ABC Company	High-tech	Brochure	$1.30	S.F.
DEF Company	Manufact.	Brochure	$ .72	L.A.
JKL Company	Manufact.	A. Report	$ .70	San Diego

FIGURE 9–3   PRINTING COMPANY B: TARGET MARKET PROFILE

Target Market Profile

Distinctive Capabilities

I. Established ability to provide high-end, color printing.

II. Established ability to turn around complex jobs with a variety of sophisticated in-house equipment.

III. Established ability to produce error free work, on-time.

IV. Established ability to provide printed materials to meet the exact requirements of the customers.

V. Established ability to maintain profitable long-term customers by combining outstanding customer service with high standards for quality requirements of the customers.

Target Market Characteristics

I. Customers' needs for high-end color printing produced on-time, with proactive communication.

II. Customers are generally more service than price-sensitive.

III. The market is focused on major corporate headquarters located on the West Coast.

IV. Competition is limited due to large format presses and in-house equipment capabilities, customer needs for high-end printing, quick communication.

V. A large market with consistently profitable characteristics, continually changing economic, and competitive factors that must be constantly monitored.

Target Prospect Group

High-tech

Manufacturing

Medical

Auto

Sample of Prospective Customers

ABC Company
GHI Company
MNO Company

DEF Company
JKL Company

PQR Company

STU Company

company's target market profile. Use worksheet F to determine your company's target market profile.

DEVELOPING TARGET PROSPECT GROUPS FROM THE TARGET MARKET PROFILE

When you have completed your target market profile for your company's target market, you will be able to begin the process of determining the companies that will make up your company's actual target prospect group(s). The process will determine which prospective customers your company will put through the Business Development Process. The group or groups of prospects your company targets can be as large as you choose. You may choose a large group of prospective customers using the criteria from your company's target market profile, or you may wish to limit the size of the group to a number you feel your marketing and sales staff can handle comfortably. You may select several groups based on different services or products your company offers, or you may choose different groups based on sales regions.

To develop a target prospect group, first decide which of the factors you have developed as part of your target market profile are the most critical element(s) to profitable business growth. For instance, say you have determined that overall margin contribution is the most critical element to a customer being profitable to your company. From your analysis, you may determine that margin per unit is a more significant element, because your company realizes better overall profits from high-margin/low-volume accounts versus high-volume/low-margin accounts.

Next, from your profile, determine the criteria you believe has the most significant relationship to the critical element(s) you've identified for your company. If you determine that overall margin dollars contributed by a customer is the critical element, you will want to analyze what criteria in your profile appears to be most related to that contribution. From the profile, it may become apparent that companies belonging to certain industries are more responsible than others for contributing to overall margin dollars. You may conclude that the

Worksheet F—Determining Target Market Profile

Target Market Profile

**Distincitve
Capabilities**

**Target Market
Characteristics**

_____
_____
_____
_____
_____
_____
_____
_____
_____
_____
_____
_____
_____
_____

_____
_____
_____
_____
_____
_____
_____
_____
_____
_____
_____
_____
_____
_____

Target Prospect Group

**Sample of Prospective
Customers**

_____

_____

_____

_____

_____
_____
_____
_____
_____
_____
_____
_____
_____
_____
_____

criteria most relevant to the critical element is customer location or a particular size range of company.

Once your company has decided what the critical element(s) of the target market profile are, and the criteria most responsible for contributing to the critical elements are set, you can begin the third step. This step begins by creating a process for identifying other companies who possess criteria and relationships to the critical elements that make up your target market profile. These companies will become prospective customers in your company's target prospect group.

Taking the time to create a target market profile and the three steps necessary to create a target prospect group will greatly increase the likelihood of prospective customers successfully moving through the Business Development Process model and into the center ring. In other words, the more care your staff puts into this part of the process, the higher the chances are that the prospective customers' needs and service requirements will match your company's distinctive capabilities.

The criteria that your company used to develop target market profiles will point you toward a group of prospective customers who possess similar critical elements and criteria. The process for identifying the prospective customers that will be part of your company's target prospect group can take many forms. To begin your company's process, your marketing and sales staff should research these different means for the most effective system of identifying prospective customers.

Research Resources

There exists a wide variety of means to research potential prospective customers. Some cost nothing but require an investment in research time. Some sources carry a high price tag, but when you weigh the accessibility and usage over several years, the cost can be considered reasonable. There are two sources of prospective customers, active and passive. Active sources of prospective customers contain large amounts of information that you or your staff actively researches. Active sources include business libraries, software databases, trade publications, and periodicals. Passive sources of prospective customers are contacted independently and through their responses qualify themselves. Passive sources include list brokers, lists brokered by trade publications, and lists developed through responses generated from trade shows or direct response marketing.

ACTIVE SOURCES

Business Directories Depending on the critical elements and criteria that make up your target market profile, different business directories can provide you with the listings of prospects you are looking for. Most of these are available at a local library. Each of these directories list companies in different groupings by size, industry, market, and affiliated associations. The directories can provide you with lists of companies, as well as addresses, phone numbers, and statistical information on revenue and employment. Some of the more well known directores include:

Industrial Marketing and Market Data Directory
Directory of Corporate Affiliations
Manufacturing USA
Moody's Industrial Manual
American Encyclopedia of Associations

Periodicals Business periodicals are an excellent source of prospective customers. For the most part, national business and trade periodicals will provide your company with larger prospective customers, dispersed nationally. However, with thorough research of these major business and trade publications, even a regionally directed company can develop a target prospect group. Throughout the year, business and trade periodicals publish a variety of features that cover different industries as well as lists of companies within specific industries. These lists include top companies based on revenue-generated, best-growth potential as measured by investment rating, fastest growing small companies, and so on. Local and regional business publications also produce regular issues of top public and private companies, as well as issues highlighting top companies in specific industries.

Major Business Periodicals

Fortune
Business Week
Inc.
Forbes
Business Journal (local and regional editions)

Trade Publications Industry-specific trade publications are published for almost every industry group imaginable. These publications can provide your marketing and sales staff with an enormous amount of information for putting together a target prospect group. To locate a trade publication for a particular industry, consult the index called *Standard Rate & Data*, available in local libraries.

Trade publications of interest to your company include those specific to your industry, more importantly those published for the industries identified within your target market profile. Unlike national business periodicals, trade publications specific to industries important to your target market profile can give your company a broad look at a range of prospects within your target prospect group. In some cases, subscriptions to trade publications are free if your company fits the profile of the trade publication's readership base.

Software Databases As information sources continue to expand, new software products are being produced that make developing a target prospect group easier. The advantage of these products is that they allow your marketing and sales staff to build a complete model of a potential group of prospective customers. The top companies in any industrial group are the easiest to find out about. These top companies are usually the most sought after by competitors. But software database products that can identify prospective customers can find the more difficult to locate middle groups of prospective customers. In addition, these products can segment the target prospect group in any number of ways.

One example of this type of product is Marketplace Business. Marketplace is produced by Marketplace Information Corporation, and uses information from Dun & Bradstreet. It is available on CD-ROM for both the Macintosh and PC compatibles. The product, which is updated quarterly, features the ability to turn your computer into a desktop resource for prospective customer lists, market research, and analysis. If, for example, your marketing and sales staff has identified several potential groups of prospective customers, your staff could choose to identify two particular eight-digit SIC codes, in four major regions. By entering into Marketplace the SIC codes, along with zip codes, area codes, city names or county names, you can produce of list of all the companies within those groups of prospective customers. To narrow the target prospect group further, your staff could then look at demographic information for the selected group. Demographic areas that would match critical elements and criteria of your target prospect profile might include number of employees, number of locations, company revenue, and so on.

PASSIVE SOURCES

List brokers Another source of prospective customers are list brokers. List brokers develop large databases of information from a broad range of sources. Using criteria such as SIC code, number of employees, annual revenue, and location, your staff can have a customized target prospect group developed. However, most list brokers are selling you the one-time rights to their list. In most cases, the list broker requires an independent mailing service to receive the list and do the mailing. Because of this, list brokers are a good source of passive development of a target prospect group.

Similarly, trade publications and trade organizations will sometimes broker their subscribers and/or members. These two sources of lists can pinpoint the exact market with many of the same critical elements and criteria as your company's target market profile. Trade publications and trade organizations can identify a specific group of prospective customers with detailed information because of their very natures. Members and subscribers give the organization or publishers detailed information upon joining the group or subscribers list. Many trade publications have highly detailed criteria for allowing companies to be part of the subscriber base. Because these subscriber lists are often audited, they represent an unusually sophisticated resource of information. As with list brokers, these organizations require that an independent mailing house receive the list and do the mailing. But if your company has accurately concluded that the critical elements and criteria from your target prospect profile are represented by this list, the percentage of return in a passive approach can be very high.

Trade shows Developing a target prospect group from response generated at a trade show is another passive approach to generating prospective customers. Trade shows present a great opportunity to gather together decision makers for the target prospect group that your company has profiled.

Your company can develop a process that allows attendees to identify themselves as potential prospects. Accomplishing this requires an integrated approach. Begin by acquiring a list of show attendees from the show management company. Then develop a mailing to the attendees that gives them a reason to stop by your booth. This can take the form of a free offer or a contest. To qualify to win, the potential prospect must complete an entry form that also doubles as a lead-qualification form. On the show floor, have additional entry/lead-generation forms available. If the offer is perceived to have value, and if your lead-generation form gives your staff the critical elements and criteria, you will have constructed a very high-quality target prospect group.

SUMMARY

To summarize, targeting is the first step of the Business Development Process. The first objective is to determine what prospective customers will make up the target prospect group. By carefully constructing a target market profile, your company can learn the critical elements and criteria that make up a profitable customer. With a profile determined, your staff can identify resources to build a target prospect group(s). This group is made up of the prospective customers that your staff has determined show the highest potential for successfully moving from the outer ring of the bull's-eye target model to the center.

Business Development Process
Step 2: Identification

The first level of the Business Development Process explained how to target industries and prospective companies within target markets. The second level will show how to initially identify the appropriate buying personnel. The objective of this chapter is to identify the correct person or persons with whom you will develop a two-way education process.

Identifying the Person with Primary Influence

The contact person you choose from within the staff of the prospective customer needs to be the primary person your company will engage in a two-way exchange of information. The correct identification is critical.

Specifically, the person you identify will need to be convinced that your company's distinctive capabilities fit the needs and service requirements of the prospective customer. During the two-way exchange of information, this individual will become educated in the features and benefits of your company's service or product. Your company will be equally dependent on this individual for the needs and service requirements of the prospective customer.

Who exactly should your company be looking for? That is not an easy question to answer. The contact may be the final decision maker, or she or he may be the person who makes the recommendation for the decision. In some companies, the person your company needs to identify is the person who will actually use the service or product. In some companies, it will be a person who is responsible for making a buying decision but will never actually use the service or product themselves.

The role of the person you are trying to identify will also vary from industry to industry. In large companies, it will be much more difficult to cut through the bureaucracy to identify the correct person.

The person your company is trying to identify is the individual who holds the primary influence in the decision to purchase your company's services or products. The individual with primary influence will set the needs and service requirements that your company's service or product must fit. When your company moves a prospective customer through the Business Development Process, you will be moving this individual of primary influence from the outer edge of the bull's-eye target model to the center.

One way to determine the job title or job function of the person you are trying to identify is to review your target market profile. Depending on the industries you have identified and the services or products your company offers, the profile of your target market may show a common role for the individual with primary influence. In many instances, the job title or job function of this individual will differ from industry to industry. Every company may differ about who the individual with primary influence will be as well as how decisions are made.

If your company has obtained a list of prospective customers that make up your target prospect group from an independent source, the list may also contain the name of the probable individual with primary influence. If the list has come from an accurately researched source, the individual with primary influence will likely be the correct person. While these lists are expensive, they may be well worth the investment in time saved.

The majority of the time when your company is developing prospective customers for a target prospect group, your staff will not know who is the individual with primary influence. To identify individuals with primary influence, your staff will have to develop a primary point of contact. The primary point of contact can be a person in a variety of job titles. It could be the receptionist in small- to medium-size companies. In medium to large companies, it could be the administrative person for a particular department where the individual with primary influence works. In some cases, the person whose job function is only to use the services and products, not to make the buying decision, can be the one who points you in the right direction. If your staff has had some experience in locating the individual with primary influence, you may seek the person who typically fills that staff role.

Job Functions of the Individual with Primary Influence

Let's look more closely at where your staff might find the individual with primary influence. Depending on the nature of the company and industry your company is targeting, the individual with primary influence may fill one of three job functions: user, manager, or buyer.

The User

The individual with primary influence might be a member of a specific department who will be the end user of your company's service or product. This individual's primary job function requires working with your service or product in order to fulfill day-to-day responsibilities. The individual will be responsible for evaluating and acquiring services or products that are necessary for the department to carry out its work function.

This is the best person to work with. More than any other representative of the prospective customer, this individual will intimately know all the details of your customer's needs and service requirements. The service or product user will also be the easiest to educate about your company's distinctive capabilities. Their level of interest regarding the features and benefits your company's service or product will offer will, in most instances, be high. More than most job functions in the prospective customer's company, the user will be most likely to see the benefits your company's distinctive capabilities have to contribute to fulfilling the user's job function.

The Manager

The second job function the individual with primary influence can hold is a manager whose department would utilize your company's service or product to accomplish the goals set out for the department as a function of the company.

In many instances, the manager will carry more authority than other individuals your company may develop a relationship with. Managers will also have a greater responsibility over the end result of using your company's service or product. The success of the manager's department may rely on how accurately your company's distinctive capabilities fit with the prospective customer's needs and service requirements. When this type of relationship can be made clear to the individual with primary influence, he or she will have a vested interest in facilitating the two-way flow of information. The more the manager can educate your company about the unique needs and service requirements of the department, and the more the manager is educated about your company's distinctive capabilities, the greater the potential benefit for both companies.

The Buyer

In the third instance, again depending on the company and industry your company is targeting, the individual with primary influence may perform a job function in a purchasing department. This person will never use your service or product. However, their primary job function is to evaluate services or products before purchase, and then negotiate the best value.

Working with the end user, the buyer will develop a set of needs, purchasing standards, and service requirements. The closer the buyer can come to fulfilling all of the needs, service requirements, and purchasing standards, the more successful the buyer will be in fulfilling his or her job function.

This circumstance requires your company to accomplish a great deal of education. Buyers tend to have a broad knowledge of many of the needs and services requirements necessary for a company to have a successful purchasing program. Their breadth of understanding is with the purchasing process, not with any particular service or product. This can be a disadvantage as well as an advantage.

The disadvantage can exist because of a lack of familiarity with and understanding of the features and benefits of the service or product. The buyer may be unfamiliar with the terms and specifications your industry uses. This situation can increase the time necessary to complete a two-way education process. Your staff will have to develop the buyer's basic understanding of terms and specifications before educating the buyer to your company's distinctive capabilities. Conversely, you will need to exhibit an awareness that confirms your understanding of the buyer's needs and service requirements.

The advantage can be that the buyer is coming into the process with few predetermined biases. This objectivity can enhance the education process, making the two-way process flow more quickly and easily. Once you have made the buyer feel confident that you have an understanding of the needs and service requirements, she or he will willingly look at how your company's distinctive capabilities can help fulfill those requirements. The buyer's level of interest regarding the features and benefits your company's service or product offer will, in most instances, be high.

The buyers will be most likely to see the benefit of using your company because your company's distinctive capabilities have best satisfied the needs, service requirements, and purchasing standards they have developed. In the end, the buyer's job function is fulfilled if the user is satisfied.

GAINING INFORMATION ABOUT THE PRIMARY CONTACT

In any of these three scenarios, it is important to know the right questions to ask. Your staff should know that the objective of this step of the Business Development Process is to identify the correct individual with primary influence, their title, direct phone line, address, fax number, and so on. It should be made clear that the objective is not to necessarily speak with the person. It is preferable not to speak to the person who holds the primary influence at this time. First, you will want to create a frame of reference, and typically that is not done by phone.

Your staff member making the inquiries needs to be familiar with the overall objective of each step of the Business Development Process. Your staff member must also have a good working knowledge of your company's service or product. In presenting himself and your company to the primary point of contact, your staff member may be asked to describe what your company does. He will need to answer in a brief manner that is understandable to someone of any variety of job levels. At the same time, he may be transferred to someone with greater responsibility or to the individual with primary influence. In this event, he will have to have a working understanding of your company's service or product and be able to represent it well over the phone.

Again, the objective is not to make contact with the individual with primary influence. The objective is to find out who that individual is. If your staff member were to inadvertently make contact with this individual with primary influence, the best course of action would be to:

➲ Identify who he is.

➲ Identify that he represents your company.

➲ Identify the service or product that your company offers.

➲ Establish that he has information he would like to send.

➲ Confirm that the individual is the correct contact.

➲ Politely end the conversation.

Five-Step Identification Process

If your staff will have to develop a primary point of contact in order to identify the individual with primary influence, you may want to establish a defined process. This process could be a series of steps. Here is an example:

Step 1

Call the prospective company and ask the receptionist for the department that would work with your company's service or product. If the company does not have a department that handles that function, the receptionist will either be the primary point of contact or will point you in the right direction.

Possible roadblock: The receptionist informs you that the company does not use your company's service or product.

Response: Ask to be connected to the purchasing department.

Step 2

When connected to the department, ask to speak to the administrative assistant.

Possible roadblock: There is no administrative assistant for the department.

Response: Ask to speak with someone in the department that would normally use your company's service or product.

Step 3

If you are connected to the admisistrative assistant, inform the him or her that your company would like to send information to the person who would work with the service or product your company supplies.

Possible roadblock:
1. The administrative assistant is unsure who that person would be.

2. The administrative assistant responds that his or her company already has a source for the service or product.

Response:
1. Suggest the job title you think the individual with primary influence would have, or ask who would be responsible for a decision on purchasing the service or product.
2. Acknowledge that they already have a source, but suggest that it would be a benefit to the decision maker to have some particular information regarding your company's service or product.

Step 4

Get the name, title, correct mailing address, direct phone number, and fax number for the individual with primary influence.

Possible roadblock:
1. The administrative assistant refuses to give out the information.

Response:
1. Ask to speak with the decision maker, or ask to be transferred to the purchasing department.
2. Identify yourself and your company's service or product, inform him that you have information you want to send him, confirm that he is the correct contact, obtain mailing information, and politely end the conversation.

Step 5

Thank him for his assistance.

Possible roadblock: You get transferred to the decision maker, the individual informs you that they are not interested in your company's service or product.

Response: Tell the individual that you understand, but you would like to send her some information you feel she may find beneficial. If she still refuses, it probably is not worth pursuing further.

Summary

To summarize the second step of the Business Development Process, the objective is to identify the person who holds the primary influence in the decision to purchase your company's services or products. We have labeled this person as the individual with primary influence. This person will set the needs and service requirements for your company's service or product. When your company moves a prospective customer through the Business Development Process, your company's staff will be moving this individual toward the center of the bull's-eye target model by developing a two-way education process.

Business Development Process
Step 3: Introduction

In this chapter, you will learn the basic elements of preliminary introduction. Through a letter and small brochure, your staff will introduce your company to the prospective customer. Your company's objective is to build a frame of reference in the mind of the individual with primary influence.

In the two previous steps of the Business Development Process, we have established a group of companies that your company will target, and your staff has identified the individuals with primary influence for each company. Now, before making an attempt to further qualify the prospective customer, a passive contact will be made.

Many sales organizations may believe that now is the time to call the individual with primary influence. Why waste the effort of mailing to the individual or, if your staff is working a target prospect group, mailing to the entire group? Why not save the postage and call to see if the prospect wants to purchase your company's service or product?

The answer is simple. The Business Development Process is designed to systematically move a group of prospective customers from the outer ring of the bull's-eye target model to the center. To market and sell smartly, the Business Development Process relies on a two-way flow of information. This exchange of information will, over time, build a relationship between the supplier and the user, where the user's needs and service requirements are exactly matched to the distinctive capabilities of the provider's service or product. The outcome is a long-term relationship. And long-term relationships are built on trust.

To build a relationship based on trust, both parties need to be receptive. A steady process that targets, identifies, and now introduces will allow a potential customer to become familiar with your company without being pushed, threatened, or misled. In the past, it may have been possible to be successful by having marketing and sales scream, "Buy me, buy me." This is no longer effective. Today, an effective process is established with the prospective customer by exchanging knowledge, then matching their needs and service requirements with your company's distinctive capabilities. As each company becomes familiar with the other through the exchange of information, a bond of trust is built.

To pave the way for a receptive environment, instead of calling, your company will now develop a tool to present a quick introduction of its distinctive capabilities and summary of services or products. This introduction needs to create a simple impression of what your company does and how it will benefit prospective customers.

Preliminary Introduction via Letter and Small Brochure

Your company's introductory package should be carefully constructed to present a brief glimpse of what you have to offer the prospect. But your company will not actually make an offer to the prospective customer in this introduction. That step will come later in the Business Development Process.

Understanding the Objective

It is critical that everyone who is working on the production of the introductory letter and small brochure have a clear objective of what each piece is trying to accomplish. As we have already stated, we are simply trying to create a frame of reference for the individual with primary influence. For example, Printing Company B's objective would be to establish a frame of reference for the individual with primary influence that they are a producer of high-quality color printing, servicing the West Coast with technology that avoids many common problems. Whether members of your company's staff will be designing the brochure and writing the text for the letter and brochure, or an outside firm produces it, everyone affiliated with the project needs to have this objective in mind.

This is the first part of the educational process. Before your company can proceed to surveying the prospective customer's needs and service requirements, the prospective customer needs to have a basic idea of who your company is and what your company can offer that would benefit their company.

CONTENTS

The letter should be brief, three to four paragraphs at most. Your company will only have a very few seconds to catch the attention of the individual of primary influence. So your company's letter must be bold and to the point. You want to make only a few points that either add to the information or emphasize a major point in the small brochure.

Who You Are The first point your company will want to get across to the prospective customer will be an explanation of who your company is. This explanation should be two to three sentences long. Your major point will detail what your company does.

Here is an example of an opening paragraph:

"I would like to take a moment to introduce my company to you. Software Company A is a rapidly growing company providing companies such as yours with automated administrative solutions."

What You Have to Offer The second point you will need to make clear is why you are writing this letter to the prospective customer. Your objective is to familiarize the prospective customer with your company. And since this is your first contact with the individual with primary influence, you may also want to fill him or her in on what you are doing. That is, you may want to state that over the next several weeks you want to inform the prospective customer about your company's distinctive capabilities as well as determine if those distinctive capabilities fit the company's needs and service requirements.

This paragraph might look like the following:

"I am writing to you because I believe that with an awareness of my company, you will see the benefits Software Company A can offer your firm. Over the next several weeks, I would like to inform you of the features and benefits of Software Company A. In addition, I would like to increase my company's knowledge of your firm's needs and service requirements. If we discover there is common ground between our companies that will be mutually beneficial, we can develop this relationship."

Industry Experience The third point you should make is the experience that your company has in providing the service or product you are offering. Your staff may feel it is important to point out how many years your company has been providing the service or product. Your staff may wish to point out some of the other companies that are your customers. Additionally, your staff may wish to emphasize a point within your company's brochure that you feel is particularly relevant to the prospective customer.

This paragraph could read as follows:

"Over the past five years, Software Company A has been an innovator in developing computer-based solutions to reduce staff administration time. In the accompanying brochure, I think you may find the example of how quickly our system can pay for itself particularly interesting. In just eight months, West Medical Clinic was able to realize a pay-back of its investment from reduced overtime."

In Closing Finally, you can inform them that you will be contacting them soon to determine their needs and service requirements. Remember, you are not necessarily looking for a response. This step is just to give the prospective customer a taste of what your company is all about. However, you will want to give the prospective customer a means to respond. You can never tell when your timing will be right on the mark; the individual with primary influence may want to talk to you immediately. Even in this competitive world, it still happens.

Figure 11–1 is a sample introductory letter.

THE BROCHURE

The small brochure typically consists of an $8^{1}/_{2}$ x 11 sheet of paper, turned lengthwise and folded in thirds. This will give your company six panels to work with, in a format that will neatly fit with the introductory letter into a standard number 10 business envelope. In the brochure, your company will have the opportunity to make a few major points. When creating the brochure, avoid the temptation of saying too much about your company. Remember, there will be opportunities to go into greater detail later in the communication process. But for now, try to limit the brochure's contents to three major points. The amount of time the individual with primary influence will spend looking at your company's brochure will be limited. Don't expect the individual to study the brochure in detail. You're not trying to make the sale here. Your company's aim is to get the attention of her or him with primary influence long enough for the letter and brochure to give her or him a frame of reference about your company.

To have the greatest impact, your company's introductory brochure should be clean, bold, and carry a clear message. This can be accomplished with concise, easy-to-read text and strong, well-defined graphics.

However your company chooses to organize the brochure, be sure to develop a set of criteria at the outset, to guarantee that the message is customer-driven. It is easy to lose objectivity when you are creating this type of communication. So, begin with the result in mind. Your staff has established what your company's distinctive capabilities are. Your company has analyzed the characteristics of your target market. Your staff has developed a profile of prospective customers within your target prospect group. Review all of this information and decide how it will contribute to producing a message that

FIGURE 11-1   SAMPLE INTRODUCTORY LETTER

SOFTWARE
COMPANY

Date

Name
Company
Address
City, State, Zip

Salutation:

I would like to take a moment to introduce my company to you. Software Company A is a rapidly growing company providing companies such as yours with automated administrative solutions.

I am writing to you because I believe that with an awareness of my company, you will see the benefits Software Company A has to offer your firm. Over the next several weeks I would like to inform you of the features and benefits of Software Company A. In addition, I would like to increase my company's knowledge of your firm's needs and service requirements. If we discover that there is common ground between the two companies, a mutually beneficial relationship can be developed.

Over the past five years, Software Company A has been an innovator in developing computer based solutions to reduce staff administration time. In the accompanying brochure, you may find the example of how quickly our system can pay for itself particularly interesting. In just eight months, the Medical Clinic was able to realize a pay-back of its investment from reduced overtime.

I will contact you the week of May 17th to discuss your needs for automating your office administration.

Sincerely,

Ron Jones
Business Development Manager

will quickly and positively give the prospective customer a frame of reference. List all of these criteria before you begin your brochure development. Then as the development of the brochure progresses, test the concept against these criteria.

Overview of Company Typically, the brochure will give the prospective customer a general overview of your company and how your company's service or product could benefit the prospective customer. The first major point for the brochure to communicate is an overview of your company. This overview should include a brief history of your company, how it is organized, and its major accomplishments. Printing Company B's overview might read:

> "Printing Company B provides corporations with high-quality full-color printing. Founded over three decades ago, the firm has grown to be one of the largest producers of annual reports on the West Coast. With offices in every major business center from Los Angeles to Seattle, Printing Company B is always close to the customer."

General Capabilities The second major point for the brochure to communicate is a summary of your company's general capabilities. This section of the brochure includes a description of your company's service or product features. In addition, you will need to detail your distinctive capabilities. Printing Company B could state:

> "Our printing facility contains the latest technology for producing both form-fed and sheet-fed printing. In addition, we are one of the few printers with the in-house capability to do color separations, binding, and die cutting."

Customer Benefits The third major point for the brochure to communicate is the benefits that your company's distinctive capabilities provide to your customers. The information in this section will come directly from the characteristics of your target market, and the profile of your target prospect group. An example of Printing Company B's approach to this point might be:

> "Our company's dedication to providing customers with the highest level of satisfaction has kept us always looking for better ways to produce printed materials. The result has been our cus-

tomers benefitting from decreased production time, increased control of quality, increased communication with the customer, and the best value for the customer's dollar."

Figure 11–2 is a sample introductory small brochure.

DON'T CLUTTER THE MESSAGE

Your introductory materials should utilize strong headlines with an economy of words. A clear, concise message will engage your readers faster, and move them to your supporting information. Photos and illustrations that quickly communicate concepts are also useful ways to get the point across. A distinct visual can build a frame of reference that will make the text of your material easier to understand. Bulleted text can also be a good method for driving a point home. Comparison charts, performance graphs, and product illustrations can instantly point out advantages to the prospective customer. Communicating a few main concepts about your company's distinctive capabilities is your objective. Remember, a picture is worth a thousand words.

SUMMARY

In summary, it should be emphasized that the more clearly your staff can communicate a customer-driven message, the more success your company will have in establishing a frame of reference for the prospective customer. In this situation, we are talking about communicating a strong, basic message as quickly as possible.

FIGURE 11–2   Sample Introductory Small Brochure

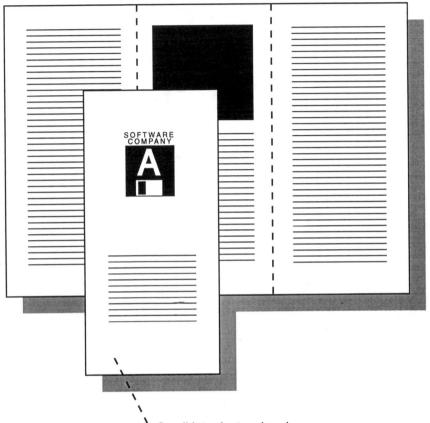

Small introductory brochure:
- Overview of company
- General capabilities
- Customer benefits

Business Development Process Step 4: Prequalification

The fourth step of the Business Development Process begins to educate your staff to the prospective customer's needs and service requirements. By phone, you will establish a preliminary needs assessment and competitor identification. Accurate and complete information will be needed to prequalify prospective customers from a requirements survey. This will lay the critical foundation to the fit/misfit model discussed earlier.

Your company's staff has several objectives from this requirements survey:

⮑ To understand the prospective customer's needs and service requirements for using your service or product.

⮑ To build a profile of your prospective customer's business.

⮑ To identify the competition.

⮑ To learn the prospective customer's criteria for selection of service or product providers.

From the information your staff obtains, they can begin to build an individual profile of the prospective customer. Then your staff will use the fit/misfit model to find holes (misfits) in the prospective customer's current service or product provider and opportunities (fits) for your service or product.

To begin, you must develop a functional form that your staff can use during a phone prequalification requirements survey. This form must be one that you are comfortable using and should evolve over time. As your staff uses it with prospective customers, test it to see how well it works during conversations with different individuals with primary influence.

DEVELOPING A SURVEY FORM

The requirements survey needs to be developed in a way that allows the individual with primary influence to pass relevant information to your company. This forum for receiving information should begin with general facts about the prospective customer. Following this first section of the survey, eight more sections are necessary. Your actual survey form may utilize some of these sections, while your staff may want to add others.

GENERAL INFORMATION

The form should begin with general information about the prospective customer:

- Contact name
- Address
- Phone number
- Fax number
- Industry type (SIC code)
- Date of interview
- Additional individuals with primary influence

CONFIRMATION OF SERVICE OR PRODUCT USAGE

The purpose of the question is to confirm the prospective customer's utilization of your type of service or product. As much as a prospective customer may have fit your target, you can't be certain the prospective customer actually uses your service or product. Or it may have its needs fulfilled internally.

Type and Description of Service or Product Used

Your staff will want to know the type and description of theservice or product being used. Are there several levels of service possible? What options are available for the product the prospective customer uses? Also, it is important to identify multiple buyers, or other locations that would use the service or product. An example might be Cellular Service Company C, which specializes in value-added phone services. In this case, Cellular Service Company C would want to know how much air time is typically used, are local or long-distance calls made, and are there multiple users of the phone service. Is this a corporate account with a fleet of phones?

Definition of How the Service or Product Is Used

Once you have established the type of service or product, you will want to get more details. How is the service or product being used? What are the channels for distribution or usage? Who is the prospective customer's client? How are the prospective customer's clients using the prospective customer's service or product?

Depending on the individual prospective customer, this information may easily flow out of a conversation. Often in the survey process, once the prospective customer has established that your purpose is to gain information, not ask for a sale, he or she will feel at ease to discuss his or her needs and service requirements.

This is one of the keys to the Business Development Process. By establishing two-way communication, a nonthreatening relationship can be established with the prospective customer. The typical marketing/sales approach is to tell the prospective customer all the great things your company does, and "do they want to buy ... please, please ... let me put you on the spot, or I'll keep nagging you until you buy." In the Business Development Process, you move with prospective customers, through the bull's-eye target, learning their needs and service requirements while educating them to your company's distinctive capabilities. As long as there appears to be a fit, you continue toward the goal of a long-term business relationship. If at any point your staff determines there is not a fit, your company drops the prospective customer from the process. In the previous example, some typical questions might be: What percentage of phone service is generally used during peak hours and off hours? What are typical call origin and destination locations? What are frequent long-distant locations served? Do the service patterns differ for these areas? Why are these service patterns used?

WHO HAS BEEN SUPPLYING THE SERVICE OR PRODUCT?

It is critical to know exactly who your competition is. With this information and a good competitor information resource file, you should be able to find a misfit, if there is one, in the prospective customer's current service or product fulfillment.

A competitor resource file can be made up of press clippings from newspapers and trade publications, competitor brochures and sales material, information obtained from your own salesforce, or customer interviews.

Some prospective customers will have several providers of a service or product. It is also important to find out which competitors are used for different needs and service requirements and why multiple providers are used. However, the trend is to move toward single vendor sourcing, so knowing all prospective customers' needs and service requirements is even more necessary.

SALES FACTORS: CRITERIA FOR SELECTING THE COMPETITOR

In painting a clear picture of the prospective customer's situation and how your company fits or fails to fit, it will become apparent what critical sales factors are important in the prospective customer's selection. Straightforward questions and answers to this issue will give you clear requirements and priorities that the prospective customer has for the service or product provider.

All industries have a minimum of at least six critical sales factors. Some of these are general to all industries, for example:

➲ Price

➲ Performance

➲ Experience

➲ Value-added features

➲ Billing

➲ Quality management program

Each industry has its own particular factors. Cellular Service Company C's customers may have network downtime as a performance factor and credit for service interruptions as a billing factor. Individual prospective customers may have critical sales factors unique to their company's needs and service requirements.

The important key here is research. This may be as simple as interviewing your own salesforce. It could include reviewing industry trade publications for articles or surveys on factors that influence prospective customers to buy. The best information will always come from prospective customers and customers themselves. Either by mail or phone, a well thought out survey of critical sales factors will give your company the most reliable information.

As your staff develops its own list of critical sales factors for your prequalification survey, remember your objectives. You are looking for a hole (misfit) in your competitor's service or product and an opportunity (fit) for your company's distinctive capabilities.

How Well Has the Competitor Been Fulfilling the Needs of the Sales Factors?

Once the prospective customer's critical needs and service requirements have been identified, your staff will need to determine how well the prospective customer's current provider fulfills those need and service requirements. In some cases, prospective customers will not be critical of their current provider. This may be out of loyalty, an unwillingness to give you an unfair advantage, or because it would be an admission of poor judgment in selecting the competitor in the first place. Nonetheless, if possible, in the context of a nonthreatening conversation, asking is worthwhile for both your company and the prospective customer. Again, you are only after information. The better the information, the better the end result for both your company and the prospective customer. From the prospective customer's point of view, the better the fit, the better the service or product conforms to their needs and service requirements. When the Business Development Process is utilized, the marketing and sales function evolves into an exchange of information that facilitates the best business relationship.

Is There a Regular Review of the Service or Product?

Many companies maintain a regular cycle of reviewing service or product suppliers. They review how their needs and service requirements have changed and how their current provider is meeting (or can meet) those needs and service requirements.

If this is the case with companies you are targeting, the timing of moving that prospective customer through the model becomes critical. It is important not to rush a prospective customer through the bull's-eye target, but to plan a specific time period in which to move the prospective customer through the process. Typically, it takes sixty to ninety days to move a prospective customer through the first ten levels. Depending on where the prospective customer is in their regular review process, you may want to alter your scheduling. If you are coming up on a review period and have not had adequate time for the proper actions, it may be more advantageous to begin the Business Development Process with your goal being the next review period. Your staff can use its review period to gain information on how best to meet the prospective customer's needs and service requirements in the next service or product review.

Some companies may review new service or product providers only when a current provider has changed its capabilities. This may include service or product failure, rate increase, change in service or product features, or the ability to meet needs and service requirements. All of these situations change the fit/misfit model and provide opportunities for your company to demonstrate how your distinctive capabilities fit the prospective customer's needs and service requirements.

Formulating questions to provide this information will allow you to plan the timing of your process. Each prospective customer will have different needs and service requirements. You will need to be able to adapt your process to meet each prospective customer's situation.

IMPORTANT FEATURES NEEDING ATTENTION

The final goal of your prequalification survey is to find any immediate needs and service requirements that need attention. At this point in your conversation, the prospective customer may be open to pointing out areas of its service or product needs where its current provider is not conforming to needs and service requirements. This is often the point where you can identify a fit for your distinctive capabilities with the prospective customer's needs and service requirements.

Figure 12–1 is a sample prequalification survey. This particular example is for Cellular Service Company C. Note how each question has been applied to the informational needs of the particular industry and the individual company. It was developed to find specific gaps in the prospective customer's current service or product provider, the definition of the prospective customer's needs and service requirements, and areas where this company's distinctive capabilities have opportunities to fit the gaps in service or product needs and service requirements that have been determined.

As your staff uses this form in actual prequalification surveys, you will no doubt modify it to better meet your company's needs. Your staff should feel free to experiment with different questions and seek different information as surveying points out the needs and service requirements of concern to your prospective customer's industry.

SUMMARY

The prequalification step is key to your staff learning the exact needs and service requirements of the prospective customers. From this step your staff will be able to build a profile of your prospective customer's business. In addition, you will be able to identify the competition for this individual prospective customer, and understand what criteria the

FIGURE 12–1   SAMPLE PREQUALIFICATION SURVEY

Prospective customer: Medical Imaging Inc.   **Interview date:** 7/15/94

Contact name: Don Smith - Purchasing Mgr.   **Industry type:** Medical

Address, City, State: 1234 NE 53rd, Fairview, NY 01191

Phone: (098)765-4321   **FAX:** (098)123-4567

Additional individuals with primary influence: George Johnson - Regional Manager

I. Confirmation of service or product usage:

Yes. The prospective customer has a sales force that uses cellular service.

II. Type and description of service or product used:

This is a corporate account that uses both local and long-distance phone calls.

III. Definition of how service or product is used:

A sales force of approximately forty are equipped with cellular phones. The phones are used in order to keep the sales force mobile. The sales force needs to keep in touch with the home office, customers, and suppliers.

IV. Who has been supplying the service or product?

The prospective customer identified two companies that they have used to provide service. The current provider is CDE Cellular Service.

V. Sales factors: criteria for selecting competitors:

The prospective customer felt that service reliability and itemized billing for each individual sales person was most important. Price was important, with the prospective customer wanting discounts for usage.

VI. How well have competitors been fulfilling sales factor?

The prospective customer felt that CDE Cellular Service was inconsistent. Billing was not set up in an itemized fashion.

VII. Is there a regular review of the service or product?

The prospective customer reviews service records of the provider every six months. If service requirements are not met, or if a new alternative presents itself, the prospective customer said they would think about making a change.

VIII. Important features needing attention:

The only thing that was mentioned by the prospective customer was the need for a discount plan based on the amount of time used.

Worksheet G—Prequalification Survey

Prospective customer: _____ Interview date: _____

Contact name: _____ Industry type: _____

Address, City, State: _____

Phone: _____ Fax: _____

Additional individuals with primary influence: _____

I. Confirmation of service or product usage:

_____
_____
_____

II. Type and description of service or product used:

_____
_____
_____

III. Definition of how service or product is used:

_____
_____
_____

IV. Who has been supplying the service or product?

_____
_____
_____

V. Sales factors: criteria for selecting competitors:

_____
_____
_____

VI. How well have compeitors been fulfilling sales factor?

_____
_____
_____

VII. is there a regular review of the service or product?

_____
_____
_____

VIII. Important features needing attention:

_____
_____
_____

prospective customer uses in selecting a vendor to provide the service or product. With this information complete, you will be able to move to the planning step of the Business Development Process.

Business Development Process Step 5: Plan

In this chapter, you will analyze the information acquired to date and develop a formal plan for future actions. Over the first four steps of the Business Development Process, your company has targeted prospective customers, identified the individual with primary influence, introduced the individual to your company, and surveyed the prospective customer's needs and service requirements. In the fifth step of the process, your staff will evaluate the information that has been exchanged to date with the prospective customer. This information needs to be analyzed then formulated into strategic planning of account-specific integrated communications. In addition, a calendar of specific dates will be applied to the account-specific plan over a sixty-day period.

Analyzing Preliminary Information

Your staff has identified a group of prospective customers that form your target prospect group. As your target prospect group reaches each ring within the Business Development Process bull's-eye target model, the fit between your company's distinctive capabilities and the prospective customer's needs and service requirements gets closer and closer. However, as more information is exchanged, your staff will begin to identify prospective customers whose needs and service requirements do not fit your company's distinctive capabilities. These companies will no longer be part of the target prospect group and will fall out of the Business Development Process. This refining of the target prospect group will allow your staff to maximize its efforts on the prospective customers with the greatest chance of producing a return.

At the fifth step of the Business Development Process, your staff has enough information to be able to assess the potential of a prospective customer. The individual with primary influence now has a frame of reference for your company. In turn, your company has prequalified the prospective customer from the information obtained in the requirements survey. From this data, along with your earlier analysis of your company's distinctive capabilities and the profile of the target market's characteristics, you can now ask—is there a potential fit?

If the potential fit exists between your company and the prospective customer, your staff will now need to formulate a set of actions for the marketing and sales team to follow. This set of actions needs to be a strategic communications plan that will produce the two-way education process necessary to take the prospective customer to the next level.

Strategically Planning Communication

First, we will discuss exactly what our objectives are in this next phase of two-way information exchange. Then, we will discuss the actions and tools that your company may use to accomplish these objectives. Finally, we will lay out a timetable to carry out the communication. This timetable will be critical in bringing the prospective customer further toward the center of the target.

Planning Objectives

Your company's objective at this level of the Business Development Process is to bring about a greater knowledge of the fit between your company's distinctive capabilities and the prospective customer's needs and service requirements.

From your company's perspective, you can ill afford to assume from the prequalification information gained in the requirements survey that your staff has a clear understanding of the important factors in doing business with the prospective customer. From the prospective customer's perspective, it has not had an opportunity to build any sort of trust in your company, understand the benefits your company can offer, or gain confidence that your staff comprehends what is required to be successful in accomplishing its business goals.

Remember, the purpose of the Business Development Process is to increase your business by building more long-term customers. In order for this process to be successful, it must be a customer-driven approach with a mutual respect for how your company's service or product can meet the needs and service requirements of the prospective customer.

Actions and Marketing Tools

In Chapter 7 we discussed the elements of integrated marketing. Now we will discuss how to use some of the elements of integrated marketing to facilitate the two-way exchange of information.

The action plans that are developed at this stage will accomplish the objectives of the next four steps in the Business Development Process. The four chapters that follow, "Awareness," "Knowledge," "Assessment," and "Proof," will go into the further details about each of these steps. But we will now preview each of these steps so you can gain an understanding of how they will fit into the planning process.

Awareness: Step 6 of the Business Development Process focuses on communication with the prospective customer. The objective of this step is to build name awareness of your company.

Knowledge: Step 7 of the process moves communication with the prospective customer to the next level beyond awareness. Specific information based on the prospective customer's needs and service requirements is communicated to build service or product knowledge.

The objective now is to help the individual of primary influence gain knowledge of your company's distinctive capabilities.

Assessment: Step 8 concentrates on increasing your company's knowledge of the prospective customer's specific needs and service requirements. Your staff's objective is to determine the prospective customer's critical requirements.

Proof: In step 9 of the Business Development Process, your company will develop information that justifies the critical needs and service requirements determined in the Assessment step. Here, the objective is to offer proof that there is a fit between your company's distinctive capabilities and the needs and service requirements of the prospective customer.

The marketing tools your staff uses and the actions they take for each of these steps will create two-way communication between your company and the prospective customer. Some target prospect groups may have similar needs and service requirements. But the likelihood of prequalification information being similar is small.

Every company will have a variety of unique features that make up the company's business needs. Because of this, your staff will have to develop strategic communication plans for every company that is part of your target prospect group. Over time, your staff will develop a series of marketing tools and actions that can be modified to meet the needs of communicating how your company's distinctive capabilities fit the needs and service requirements of prospective customers.

TIMING

The strategic communications plan defines the actions your marketing and sales team can follow. During a specific period of time, which your staff will define, your company needs to build the prospective customer's awareness of and trust in your company. The prospective customer also needs to develop a knowledge of what benefits your company can offer. In addition, the prospective customer must gain confidence that your staff realizes what needs and service requirements are critical to achieving its business goals.

This can only be accomplished over a defined period of time. The timing of your company's actions is crucial to the success of the strategic communication plan. If too much information is exchanged too quickly, general conclusions will be drawn by both your company and the prospective customer. If information is exchanged over too broad a time period, continuity will be lost. For two-way education to actually evolve, bits of information need to be built upon each other. In order for this education process to take place within the Business Development Process, these bits of information need to be exchanged in a strategic manner. Each step of the strategic communication plan should be executed with a precise purpose and timing. Every action should increase the education of your company to the needs and service requirements of the prospective customer and increase the prospective customer's knowledge of your company's distinctive capabilities.

The strategic communications plan provides a timetable to accomplish this. The actual time it takes to build these types of relationships will vary from prospect to prospect. Some prospective customers may quickly gain a knowledge of your company's service or product. They may be in a position to understand quickly the benefits that a fit between your company's distinctive capabilities and their needs and service requirements will bring to their company. Unfortunately, few prospective customers will be waiting for you to contact them. In most situations, they will have already established vendor relationships.

As part of the strategic communication plan, a standard timetable needs to be developed. This standard timetable then can be modified as needed. The timetable should allow for building name awareness, gaining service or product knowledge, assessing critical requirements, and developing proof of a fit between distinctive capabilities and the prospective customer's needs and service requirements. In most cases, this will take between eight and twelve weeks. You may want to start with a ten-week process, adjusting it as your staff gains experience.

The timetable is broken down into four parts. The first part will be to establish name awareness. Establishing name awareness and confirming that the prospective customer is receptive will take the first five weeks. The second part will create an in-depth knowledge of the service or product your company offers. We will assume that this will take three weeks. The third part will be an assessment of the critical requirements of the prospective customer. It will take one week to determine these requirements. The final part will be to develop proof that your company's distinctive capabilities meet the needs and service requirements of the prospective customer.

Figure 13–1 illustrates a sample strategic communication plan. On page 156 is a blank worksheet (worksheet H) your company can use to develop your own strategic communication plans.

Managing the Planning Process

The strategic communication plan must be well managed to be successful. A well-designed plan needs to be implemented by a marketing and sales team that will take responsibility for producing the communication tools and taking the appropriate actions as planned.

Different companies will progress at different rates through the Business Development Process. This will require that someone takes responsibility for keeping track of what communication has taken place and the result of the actions. From the point a prospective customer is targeted, this individual will need to keep a detailed record of information collected from the Identification and Prequalification steps. In addition, a record needs to be kept of the communication pieces that have been sent to the prospective customer: letters, brochures, and other information. Finally, because a team of people will be involved in process, communication between all participants is essential.

Determining the Marketing and Sales Team

The marketing and sales team your company assembles to administer the strategic communication plan needs to be able to produce materials and take the actions that are necessary to make the plan successful. If your company has a small staff, outside services may be needed to produce some of the materials, but as long as the scope of your effort is defined by the size of your team, it is possible to be very successful. In determining the team of individuals, think about the variety of

FIGURE 13–1 SAMPLE of STRATEGIC COMMUNICATION PLAN

Strategic Communication Plan

Prospective customer: Medical Imaging Inc.

WHEN	STEP	WHAT	WHO
WEEK 1 Date	Awareness 7/11/94	Starter kit/Cover letter	Joan
WEEK 2 Date	Awareness 7/18/94	Direct Mail	Joan
WEEK 3 Date	Awareness 7/25/94	Service overview	Joan
WEEK 4 Date	Awareness 8/2/94	Article reprint	Joan
WEEK 5 Date	Awareness 8/9/94	Phone call/Confirm receptiveness	Rob
WEEK 6 Date	Knowledge 8/16/94	Capabilities brochure/Cover letter	Joan
WEEK 7 Date	Knowledge 8/23/94	Service specific one-page sheet	Joan
WEEK 8 Date	Knowledge 8/30/94	Value-added suggestion book	Joan
WEEK 9 Date	Assessment 9/16/94	Phone assessment	Rob
WEEK 10 Date	Proof 9/13/94	Audio/Visual simulation	Joan

WORKSHEET H—DETERMINING A STRATEGIC COMMUNICATION PLAN

Strategic Communication Plan

Prospective customer: _____

WHEN	STEP	WHAT	WHO
WEEK 1 Date	**Awareness** _/_/_		
WEEK 2 Date	**Awareness** _/_/_		
WEEK 3 Date	**Awareness** _/_/_		
WEEK 4 Date	**Awareness** _/_/_		
WEEK 5 Date	**Awareness** _/_/_		
WEEK 6 Date	**Knowledge** _/_/_		
WEEK 7 Date	**Knowledge** _/_/_		
WEEK 8 Date	**Knowledge** _/_/_		
WEEK 9 Date	**Assessment** _/_/_		
WEEK 10 Date	**Proof** _/_/_		

functions that need to be performed. These functions include: letter writing, telemarketing, administration, sales strategy, product development, pricing, service, and marketing strategy. Depending on your company and its structure, you may already have departments that can fill these roles.

Your company will probably need to produce marketing communications pieces. When you structure your plan, you may determine that your company already has some of the pieces you will need. However, in most cases your staff will need to prepare the different communications pieces. The complexity of these projects will vary depending on the function of the piece. These materials can range from an introductory letter to a capabilities brochure. You may have the ability on staff to design and write marketing materials. If you do not, you will need to consult with a freelancer who has the necessary capabilities or hire a design/marketing/advertising company.

The team will also need participants who have the skills and comfort level necessary to interview the prospective customers. A warm, sincere personality that will not intimidate the prospective customer will generally be the most successful. The individual who makes the assessment of the prospective customer needs to have some sales savvy and service or product knowledge. As this person develops a dialogue with the prospective customer, he or she will have to pursue areas of interest and be able to anticipate opportunities that may uncover the fit between your service or product and the prospective customer's needs and service requirements. For example, as the sales team for Printing Company B develops a dialogue with a prospective customer, they may find that the prospective customer is interested in the speed and quality mentioned by the printer. From a discussion of past projects, the sales team feels that an opportunity exists to fit the printing company's distinctive capabilities to the customer's need for meeting deadlines without sacrificing quality standards.

A team member must coordinate the action plans. This person will need to manage the schedule of actions that the strategic communication plan has laid out. It is up to this person to assign all tasks necessary to complete all actions set forth in the strategic communication plan. This individual will have to make sure that all necessary materials have been produced. He or she must coordinate the customizing of communication pieces to fit the individual prospective customer. It is this person's responsibility to initiate the mailing of marketing materials per the plan. He or she will also have to verify that team members have made the scheduled calls required to acknowledge receptiveness of the prospective customer and conducted the necessary interviews to assess the critical requirements of the prospective customer. The individual who coordinates the strategic communications plan will also be responsible for keeping a record of the results of all completed action for each individual prospective customer.

The marketing and sales team will also need members who function as coaches. Coaches will be marketing and sales personnel with experience in managing accounts, who can advise the coordinator on future actions necessary to match your company's distinctive capabilities to the needs and service requirements of the prospective customer. Service and product knowledge as well as production or operations experience will greatly help these individuals advise the team. A coach for Printing Company B might suggest sharing a profile history of a previous printing project with a similar type of company that demonstrates both speed of production and a flawless final piece.

TRACKING

The complexity of managing the strategic communication plan will depend on the number of companies that make up your target prospect group. Also, the variety of different levels of progress made with individual prospective customers through the strategic communication plan will increase the need to manage the target prospect group.

Tracking can be accomplished in a variety of ways. The simplest method is to use a form similar to the example of a strategic communication plan. The form will keep track of important information regarding each individual company within the target prospect group. Your staff will want to include what action was taken, what member of the marketing and sales team was responsible for conducting the action, the date the action took place, and the result of the action that was taken. Your staff may want to include an area to record information discovered about the prospective customer during any action step, to help in building a database of prospective customer needs and service requirements. Finally, the form should be flexible enough to accommodate any modification to the strategic communications plan. As information is exchanged with the prospective customer, your team may decide that the strategic communication plan needs to be altered to best illustrate the fit that exists between your company and the prospective customer.

Automation is another method for keeping track of strategic communication plans. An automated method utilizing computer software can save time in determining the progress of prospective customers. Having this information on a computer also makes it easier for all members of the team to access.

A variety of computer databases exists to keep track of notes and status information for the strategic communication plan. Also, marketing and sales automation software can be adapted to serve this function. If your company has a network that this information can be kept on, remote members of the marketing and sales team can keep up to date on action assignments and the result of other team member's actions. (See Chapter 8 for additional information on contact management software.)

TEAM COMMUNICATION

Whether your marketing and sales team is large or small, it is important for all members to be continuously informed of the status of the strategic communication plan. The individual team member who has been assigned responsibility for managing the plan will also need to be responsible for communication.

There are many reasons why good communication is important. The most obvious is that all members of the marketing and sales team are aware of when they need to execute the part of the plan for which they have responsibility. Good communication is also important for the quick relaying of results from actions taken. This can be crucial to your team's ability to be flexible in modifying communication pieces and information to fit the prospective customer's requirements. The benefit of good communication can also come about from the insights of team members, particularly those with coaching functions, about the information coming back from the prospective customer. Good communication can often result in speeding up the process as well as creating a tighter fit between the companies.

SUMMARY

The Planning step of the Business Development Process gives your company an understanding of how to create a strategic communication plan. Managing the planning process with effective tracking and communication, as well as having a marketing and sales team made up of individuals who can help your company find ways to show that a fit exists between your company and the prospective customer, are critical components to success. Now we can move on to a more detailed look at each of the Business Development Process steps that make up the plan.

PART IV

COMMUNICATION

BUSINESS DEVELOPMENT PROCESS
STEP 6: AWARENESS

In Part III, you learned how to target a group of prospective customers, identify the individual with primary influence, create a frame of reference through an introduction, prequalify prospective customers by learning their needs and service requirements, and plan a schedule for communicating to prospective customers. Part IV will discuss how to communicate with prospects. The objective of this chapter is to show how to build name awareness for your company.

Raising the Level of Name Awareness

Before any prospective customer can even consider doing business with your company, it must first expand its frame of reference. Your marketing and sales staff should assume that a new prospective customer has little or no awareness of your company. If a prospective customer does have an awareness of your company, your staff has no way of knowing if that awareness is accurate. The prospective customer may be associating your company with something a competitor of yours said. It may have known an associate who gave it his or her perspective on your company. It may have drawn an inaccurate impression from something its staff members read about your company.

Regardless, your staff should assume there is little or no awareness. This will allow your staff to create an accurate perception.

What exactly is name awareness? What level of name awareness are you looking for? Beyond a basic frame of reference, name awareness is a prospective customer's ability to associate your company's name with a particular service or product.

Before the Introduction step, a prospective customer of Software Company A would only have the awareness that a company called Software Company A is in the software business. After a frame of reference has been created, the prospective customer should recall that Software Company A produces medical software. Now, Software Company A will send a series of communication pieces to the individual with primary influence. Its objective is to create a perception of who Software Company A is and what market they serve. If it is successful over a defined period of time, the individual with primary influence will have a name awareness of Software Company A. The prospective customer will associate the name of the software company with a product that uses software to automate the administration functions of specialized medical practices.

Types of Communications

In this chapter, we will discuss five actions that can be taken to raise the prospective customer's level of awareness. These actions include sending communications material that you can adapt for your company and its particular industry. These are only suggested materials. Your company may have other communication materials that can serve the same function. Or, as your marketing and sales staff gain experience in applying the Business Development Process, they may experiment with different types of marketing material. Whichever the case, as long as the objective being described is reached, there is a broad array of material that can serve this function.

The five actions described in this chapter are designed to be implemented over a five-week period. Each of the five actions builds bits of information upon each other to expand the prospective customer's frame of reference that was created with the Introduction in

Step 3. We will begin by creating a starter kit and cover letter that your staff can use to introduce your company's service or product. Next we'll discuss the development of a direct-mail piece that will highlight what your company does. A general service or product description overview follow-up piece will serve as the next action. An article reprint or third-party endorsement will be used as the next action to serve as a testimonial. Finally, your staff will confirm the receptiveness of the individual with primary influence.

STARTER KIT/COVER LETTER

The starter kit serves two purposes. First, it is a communication tool to inform the prospective customer of your company's intentions. Your staff will use the cover letter to tell the individual with primary influence the process your company is going through. Second, with the starter kit you will give the prospective customer the opportunity to respond to your staff. Should the individual with primary influence realize the immediate need for your company's service or product, she or he has a means to initiate the business relationship.

Cover Letter The cover letter should contain three basic messages. These messages should be concise, simply worded, and easy to read.

The first message introduces your company. It should contain a statement positioning your company within your industry. A statement should also inform the prospective customer that you are eager to assist them in discovering more about your company. Another statement should describe the materials that you are including with the letter. This should state that you do not necessarily expect them to use the material right away; however, the kit is a demonstration of your company's interest in doing business with the prospective customer. Cellular Service Provider C's cover letter could read:

"Cellular Service Provider C is one of the premier service providers in the mobile communication industry. Our staff is eager to assist you in learning about our company. For your convenience, a personalized file folder containing a service order form, rolodex card, and service instructions has been included. Although you may not need to use these materials now, we want them to be convenient for you at a moment's notice."

The second message will detail the process: Over a specific time period, the prospective customer will become acquainted with your company's capabilities and approach to doing business. Your staff may also want to include a statement informing the individual with primary influence what you would like them to do with the material if it is of interest to them. Also include a statement explaining that your company is interested in exploring if the two companies' business needs match. It is important not to build an adversarial relationship, where you are chasing down the prospective customer. The statement should have a nonthreatening flavor. This is consultative selling, where your company is exploring to see if there is a match that will benefit both companies. Cellular Service Company C's letter would continue:

"Over the next few weeks, you will be hearing more about our company's capabilities. When you receive something of interest, place it in your file folder and we can discuss it at your earliest convenience. Our company wants to learn more about your firm and whether our capabilities meet your needs."

The third message is a testimonial. This will include a statement about other customers that your company's service or product has benefited. You may wish to list several that may be familiar to the prospective customer. In closing, the staff member who will sign the letter should state that your company is looking forward to developing a relationship with the individual with primary influence. Also include a statement that your company is looking forward to exploring opportunities that will mutually benefit both companies.

Starter Kit There are a lot of possible materials that can make up your company's starter kit, depending on your company's service or product. While these items will vary a great deal from company to company, the following will describe some possibilities. Your staff should use these as a starting point for developing your own starter kit.

To begin with, include a folder that the prospective customer can use to organize the materials your company sends them. This can be a simple, colored paper folder that your staff has labeled with your company's name. The other extreme is a customized plastic folder that has been imprinted with your company's name, logo, and marketing tag line.

The next element the starter kit should contain is a contact information item. This gives the prospective customer a means of contacting your staff, either immediately or in the future, when they are interested in pursuing your service or product. A minimal approach would be to include the business card of your staff member who has been assigned responsibility for the prospective customer. A more sophisticated approach would be to include a rolodex card with all contact information included. Another effective approach is to include a plastic card, in a shape and size similar to a credit card. The card would contain your company's name, logo, and contact information. This card can be personalized with the prospective customer's company name, and even a customer account number can be assigned.

The third item that should be included in the starter kit is an order initiation form. This item may vary from company to company, depending on the service or product. Basically, your staff should include some means for the prospective customer to respond in the future when it is ready to request services or place an order for products. This can be a service order form or a purchase order form. Your company may already have forms of some kind that are used by a customer in doing business. In addition to whatever form your staff chooses to use, your company should include a separate instruction device. This can be a simple sheet that lists step-by-step instructions for using your service or product. Your staff may want to use a more detailed format. This is fine, but be very cautious not to drop too much information on the prospective customer now! There will be opportunities later in the process that are more appropriate for in-depth details on using your service or product. A four-to-five page booklet is appropriate, but save a service or product guide for later. Your objective is to give the prospective customer a simple means to respond down the road. Overwhelming the customer with information now will be counterproductive to the Business Development Process. Figure 14–1 shows a sample of a starter kit and cover letter.

Figure 14–1 Starter Kit/Cover Letter

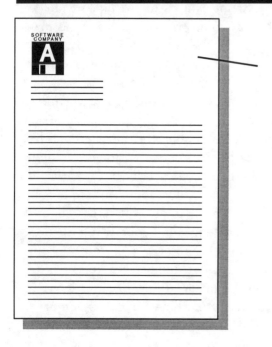

Inform the prospective customer that you will be helping them learn about your company.

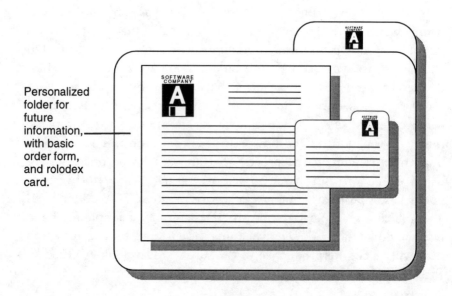

Personalized folder for future information, with basic order form, and rolodex card.

Direct Mail

The direct mail piece has two purposes. First, in broad terms, the direct mail piece communicates the benefits of your company's service or product. Second, it gives the prospective customer a vehicle to specify its areas of interest in your company's service or product.

The secret with direct mail is to intrigue the recipient from the moment he or she receives the piece. But the direct mailer can't stop there; it must hold the recipient's interest as he or she opens the piece and reviews the information, and then it must motivate him or her to respond to the offer.

This means that on the outside of the piece, whether an envelope or a self-mailer, the direct mailer should contain some message that will be of a particular interest to the individual with primary influence. The key here is to have a simple and direct message, which functions as a teaser. For instance you may pose a question, the first part of a thought, an intriguing fact, or a provocative statement. Whichever your staff chooses, the objective is to get the recipient to open the mailer.

When the prospective customer opens the mailer, you need to hit him or her with a bold statement that motivates him or her to read the supporting text. This statement can either complete the thought, answer the question, or relate to the fact stated on the outside of the mailer. In either case, this main statement needs to relate to the general capabilities of your company's service or product.

It is important in the development of any direct mail piece that your company produces it with a customer-driven motivation. That is, any statement must quickly make the recipient recognize that he or she will realize benefits as a result of responding to your offer.

All text that follows your main statement needs to be in support of the benefits the prospective customer will realize. When preparing this text, your staff should keep in mind that you will not have the recipient's attention for long. Therefore, your staff will want to use concise, well-worded text. Economy of words, bulleted text, and the strategic use of subheads to move the reader through the mailer will all add to its success.

Finally, the prospective customer should be led to the offer your direct mail piece is presenting. This offer allows your prospective customer to specify its areas of interest and to request more information and details about your company's capabilities.

This is one of the most important functions *direct mail* offers. The structure of direct mail allows for the two-way exchange of information. Your company attempts to get the prospective customer interested. If you are successful, the prospective customer asks you to respond back to them. In addition, the response will usually help add to your company's knowledge of the prospective customer's needs and service requirements.

It is not necessary for the prospective customer to respond to the direct mail piece. If they do not respond, don't delete them from the process. As part of your strategic communication plan, your company's objective in using the direct mailer is to raise the prospective customer's awareness of your company. This may be accomplished without the prospective customer requesting more information at this time. Consider yourself several steps ahead of the game if your company does get a response. There is now more evidence that a fit may exist between the two companies.

On the following page is an example of a fairly generic direct mailer. The envelope contains a simple teaser, "Ever wonder..." When the direct mailer is opened, its main statement completes the envelope statement, "Just What Can We Do For You?" Within the direct mail piece, the interior headline "Here Are Just A Few Things" and the text that follows support the main statement. The text gives an overview of the capabilities and benefits that will be realized from the capabilities. A business reply card contains the offer, and is the vehicle for response. The business reply card should contain an area where your staff can request information about the prospective customer. Completing this information then appears to be a requirement as part of the prospective customer's request for more information about your company. See Figure 14–2.

General Service or Product Description

The next action should build on the two previous awareness action steps taken as part of the strategic communication plan. The starter kit informs the prospective customer of your company's intentions.

FIGURE 14–2   DIRECT MAIL PACKAGE

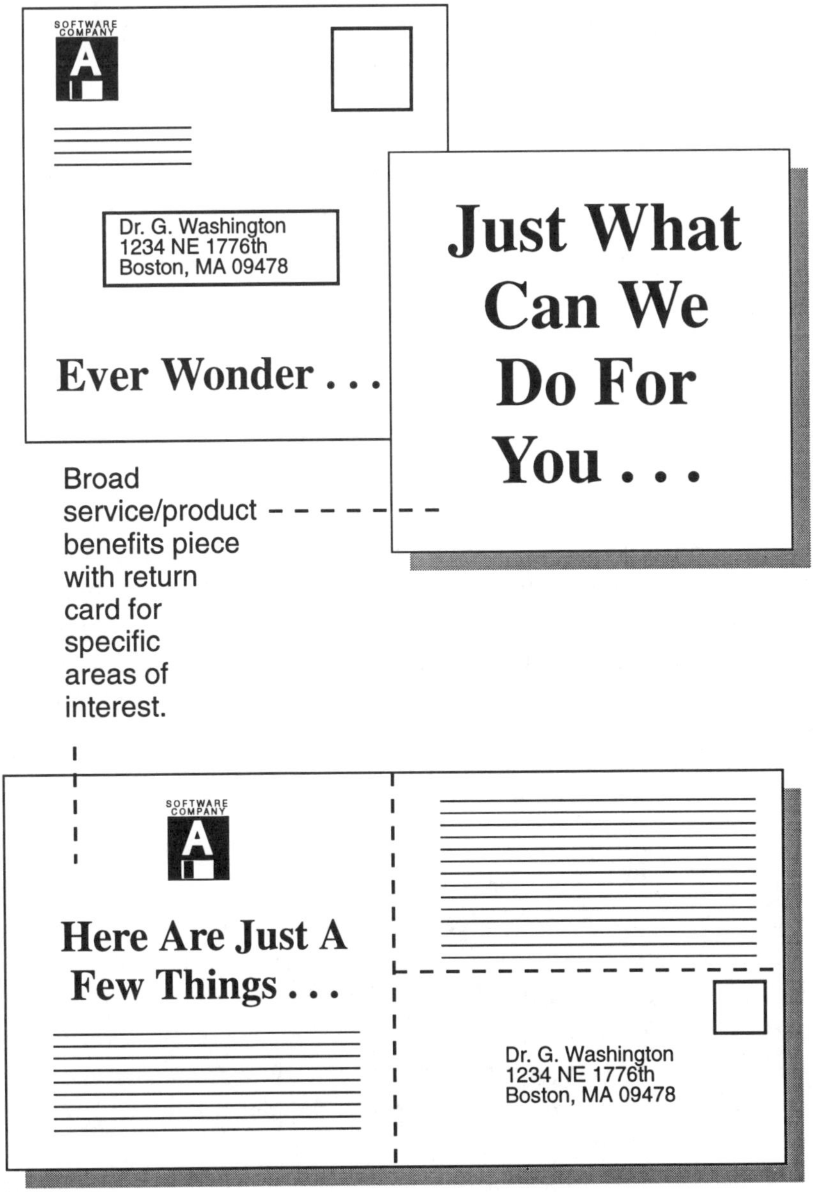

SOFTWARE COMPANY

A

Dr. G. Washington
1234 NE 1776th
Boston, MA 09478

Ever Wonder . . .

Just What
Can We
Do For
You . . .

Broad
service/product
benefits piece
with return
card for
specific
areas of
interest.

SOFTWARE COMPANY

A

Here Are Just A
Few Things . . .

Dr. G. Washington
1234 NE 1776th
Boston, MA 09478

You used the direct mailer to communicate a broad overview of your company's capabilities. Both items gave the prospective customer the opportunity to respond to your staff. Now your staff will develop an informational piece that explains or demonstrates your company's commitment to service or the quality of your product.

The general service or product description should add to the prospective customers' frame of reference. To accomplish this, it should inform the prospective customer of your company's ability to produce a service or product that has demonstrated its ability to meet the needs and requirements of your company's current customers.

As it is still early in the strategic communication plan, your company should keep this action simple. This should be a general information piece that builds on the awareness of your company without going into too much detail. The amount of material should also be kept to a reasonable length. Four pages maximum and a cover letter are generally adequate.

The form of material your company develops will fall into one of three types: product catalog, directory of offices, or service overview.

Product Catalog A product catalog should consist of brief descriptions and an illustration of your company's line of products. If your company's product line is limited to only one or two products, the catalog might, for instance, show an illustration or photo of the entire product, then break down the major elements of the product and give a brief description of the functions of each one.

Directory of Offices If your company relies on a network of offices to meet the needs and service requirements of your customers, a directory or map will be an effective way to illustrate this commitment to customer service. This may not require that your company have a large nationwide network of offices. If your company is regionally based, showing its service coverage areas may also be an effective means to present your company's accessibility.

Service Overview A service overview booklet briefly explains and diagrams the services your company offers. This could incorporate your services as a whole, or it could break down the services your company offers into elements of service. Each element of service could be described and illustrated, with a summary description showing how all the elements fit into your company's capabilities.

Cover Letter A cover letter should accompany this general service/product overview, to set the stage for the recipient. At this point in the strategic communication plan, your staff wants to explain why they are sending the item to the prospective customer. The cover letter becomes an opportunity to build on the relationship with the individual with primary influence.

The cover letter should include three clear messages. Depending on what type of piece your staff has chosen as its general service or product description, the information will vary. However, in general terms these three main messages should be similar.

The first message should reinforce the contents of the material your staff is including. If for example your staff has sent a directory of offices, the message might begin with a statement about the strength of your company's network of coverage. A statement should follow as to why that is of importance in customer-driven terms.

The second message should indicate to the prospective customer why your company feels it is important for the individual with primary influence to be aware of the information. There should also be a second statement that states your company's commitment to providing service or products that meet the needs and service requirements of your customer.

The third message should give an example of how your company's services or products have benefited other customers. If possible, you may want to use an example from the same industry that the prospective customer is part of. In closing, your staff should simply state its intentions of applying its service or product to meet the prospective customer's needs and service requirements. Figure 14–3 shows a sample general service or product description layout.

Article Reprints (Third-Party Endorsement)

The article reprint serves one main purpose. A testimonial from an outside party will provide more credibility than any statement your company can produce. It is particularly important to establish an outside endorsement at this point in your strategic communication plan.

Figure 14–3 General Service or Product Description

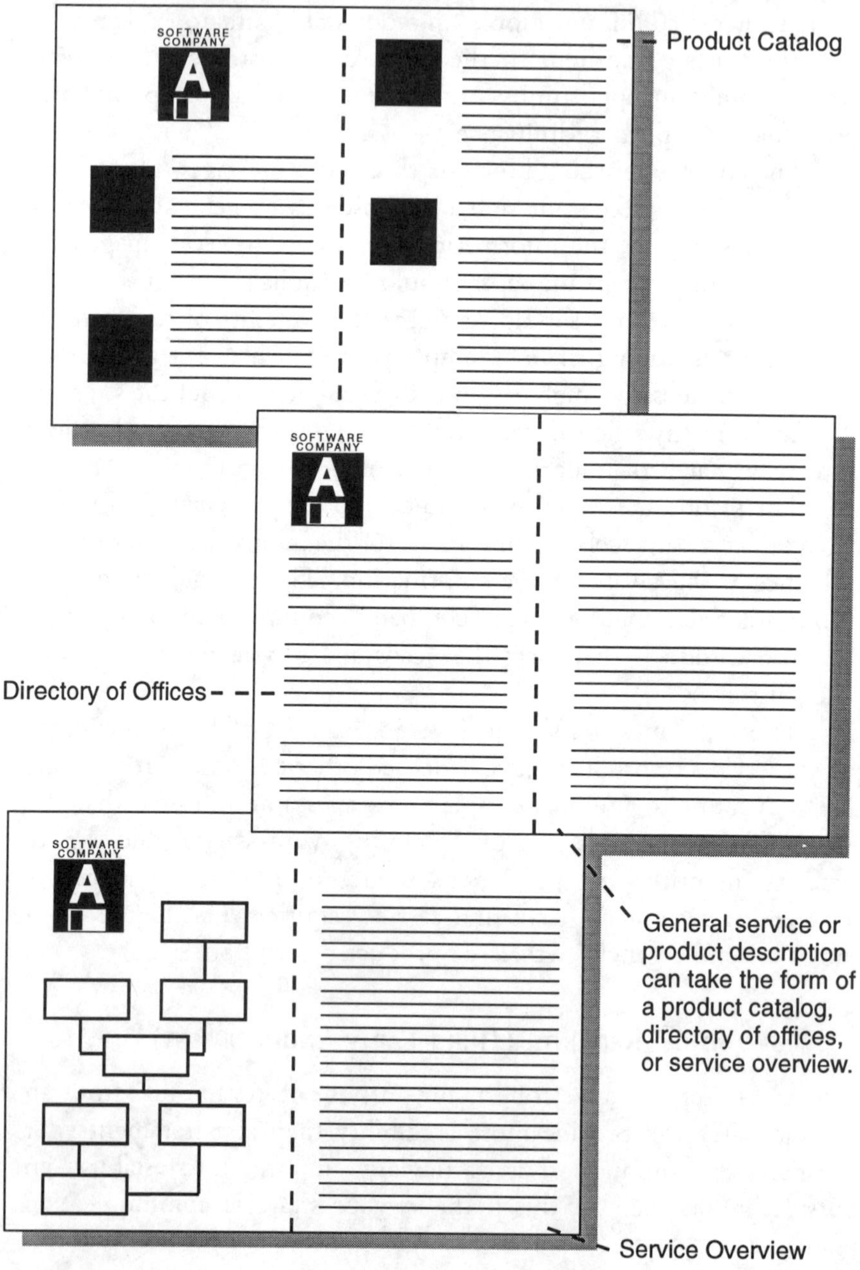
Product Catalog
SOFTWARE COMPANY
A
Directory of Offices
SOFTWARE COMPANY
A
SOFTWARE COMPANY
A
General service or product description can take the form of a product catalog, directory of offices, or service overview.
Service Overview

Building awareness for your company's capabilities through an article reprint will give the prospective customer a different perspective on your company.

Your marketing and sales team probably have a collection of articles that have been published in magazines or trade publications. These articles can be reviews of new products, evaluations of new service innovations, or recognition that has been awarded to your company. Articles that compare your company's service or product with your competitors can be a powerful tool in gaining the awareness of the prospective customer.

If your staff feels your company does not have the appropriate articles, it is necessary to begin a process to produce them immediately. To begin the process, your staff should develop a series of press releases that announce new products, product improvements, new services, or service innovations. In addition, publications in your industry may have awards for customer service or product innovation. While these awards are nonbiased and the publications that give them can not be influenced, a well-organized public relations effort can put your company in a much better position to be recognized.

The article reproduction should be of similar quality to the original. Most publications will reproduce articles, including the cover, for a reasonable fee. This is especially attractive if the article includes photos or illustrations of your company's product. If the article is only in black and white, less expensive reprints can be produced. Figure 14–4 shows the layout of an article reprint.

Phone Call to Confirm Receptiveness

At this point in the strategic communication plan, your company has three purposes in confirming receptiveness: confirmation, assessment, and understanding.

Confirmation: The first purpose is to confirm that the information your staff has been sending has been received. Also, your staff will want to confirm that the correct individual with primary influence has been contacted.

Assessment: The second purpose is to determine the prospective customer's awareness of your company. By asking a few questions

Figure 14–4   Article Reprint

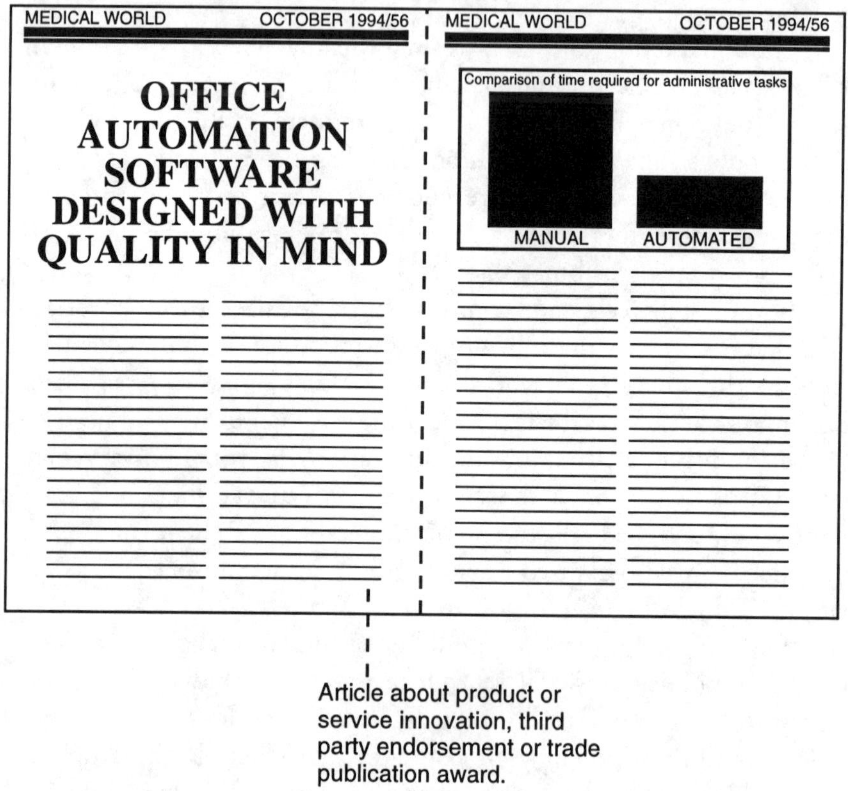

MEDICAL WORLD   OCTOBER 1994/56

OFFICE AUTOMATION SOFTWARE DESIGNED WITH QUALITY IN MIND

MEDICAL WORLD   OCTOBER 1994/56

Comparison of time required for administrative tasks

MANUAL   AUTOMATED

Article about product or service innovation, third party endorsement or trade publication award.

pertaining to the capabilities of your company, your staff should be able to subjectively assess if the individual with primary influence is associating your company's name with your company's capabilities.

Understanding: The third, and most important, purpose of confirming receptiveness is the opportunity it gives your staff to learn more about the prospective customer's specific needs and service requirements. For the most part, the Awareness step has been your company's opportunity to educate the individual with primary influence. Every opportunity for your company to be educated by the prospective customer must be taken advantage of if a fit is to be realized. A two-way education process will result in a mutually beneficial business relationship.

What is the best way for your staff to accomplish this action step of confirming receptiveness? To begin with, the staff member who has been assigned responsibility for this particular prospective customer will need to contact the individual with primary influence. In almost every case, this will be done by phone. In a few cases, if the prospective customer is in the same location as your staff, this could be done in person. However, this may be too pushy for most prospective customers at this point in the Business Development Process. An exception is if the individual with primary influence responds to one of the pieces of communication.

The member of your staff who will be making the contact needs to feel comfortable with the action. It is beneficial if this person has telemarketing experience, sales experience, or commands a high degree of service or product knowledge and confidence. As we have already detailed, the staff member will have three objectives in the call. During the conversation, the staff member will have to get verification that the materials have reached the correct person. He or she will have to get a sense of the degree to which the prospective customer has associated your company's name with your company's general capabilities. Also, your staff member should be prepared to ask specific questions, with the intention of discovering more about the particular requirements of the prospective customer.

In most cases, this phone call will end up being very conversational. Once your staff member has identified herself and made it clear that her intention is just to get a sense of the prospective customer's impressions and expectations in doing business, not to hard sell them, the individual with primary influence generally is quite comfortable in a discussion. Once the tone of the call has become conversational, your staff member can manage the conversation, rather than quiz the prospective customer.

SUMMARY

Your staff's purpose in the Awareness step of the Business Development Process is to increase the prospective customer's association of your company's name with the general capabilities your company offers. The process of building awareness needs to be completed over a defined period of time. This will enable the individual with primary influence to have their perception shaped by a series of communication pieces that your staff develops. The communication pieces begin sending a very simple message, with each piece giving a fuller picture of the benefits your capabilities can provide to customers. Every item presented to the prospective customer includes some means for the individual with primary influence to respond to should they feel there is an immediate need for more details regarding your service or product. The objective is not necessarily to get a response. The objective is to raise the name awareness of your company by educating the prospective customer about your capabilities.

With the Awareness step of the Business Development Process accomplished, receptiveness can be confirmed. The next step will be to use more defined communication to take the prospective customer to the next level—a knowledge of your company's distinctive capabilities.

Business Development Process Step 7: Knowledge

This chapter is designed to take communication with the prospective customer to the next level beyond awareness. In the previous chapter, you learned how to use general information to educate the individual with primary influence and gain name awareness. Now, you will be communicating specific information based on the prospective customer's requirements to build service or product knowledge. Your staff's objective is to help your prospective customer gain knowledge of your company's distinctive capabilities, specifically as it applies to its needs and service requirements.

Developing the Prospective Customer's Understanding of Your Company's Distinctive Capabilities

If your company is to be considered a long-term service or product supplier, the prospective customer must now develop a deeper understanding of your company's distinctive capabilities. From your marketing and sales staff's confirmation of the individual with primary influence's receptiveness, your staff will need to take specific actions to increase the prospective customer's general awareness of your company's capabilities. There can be no confusion about what your company can do to benefit the prospective customer.

For example, the prospective customer may have developed an awareness that a printing company exists call Printing Company B. Printing Company B has communicated with the prospective customer several times as part of a strategic communication plan to create awareness. The individual with primary influence now thinks of Printing Company B as a company that serves the West Coast, with full-color printing. This perception that the prospective customer has gained is enough to accomplish the objectives of Printing Company B's Awareness step.

After the Knowledge step, the prospective customer will have gained an understanding that Printing Company B uses a variety of sophisticated in-house equipment to produce high-end color printing. The individual with primary influence has learned that Printing Company B uses proactive communication and automated technology to produce error-free work, on time. In addition, he or she has seen evidence of Printing Company B's reputation for meeting customer needs and service requirements and for establishing long-term relationships.

So, the objective of the Knowledge step of the Business Development Process will be to use more defined communication to take the prospective customer to the next level—a knowledge of your company's distinctive capabilities. Your staff will emphasize specific information about your company's service or product as it applies to prospective customers' needs and service requirements.

Types of Communication

In this chapter, we will examine the three actions that should occur in order to build the prospective customer's depth of knowledge. As companies and industries vary, these communication materials should be considered suggestions that your staff can modify to meet your company's needs. Your company may already have communication materials that can be used for these same purpose. Your staff may want to experiment with different types of marketing material to see which is most successful. There are many different kinds of materials that can be used to reach the objectives described here.

Over a three-week period, your staff should accomplish the three actions described in the Knowledge step. Information from these three actions continues to be assembled as part of the two-way education process. First, to expand the prospective customer's knowledge of your company's service or product, your company will send a major capabilities brochure and cover letter. A data/product sheet and cover letter will then be developed that details your company's specific services or products. Next you will send a value-added suggestion booklet for your prospective customer to use in evaluating its service or product needs.

Major Capabilities Brochure/Cover Letter

The two elements that make up this package of communication materials are perhaps the most important to consider in the entire strategic communication plan. Your company's capabilities brochure and the cover letter that accompanies it will have the greatest educational effect on the individual with primary influence. A variety of elements can make up a capabilities brochure. Like other communications material we have discussed, the actual contents will vary a great deal with individual companies and industries. However, the capabilities brochure needs to create a deep knowledge of your company's distinctive capabilities. Depending on the similarities of the prospective customers in your target prospect group, your staff may want to include customer-driven benefits that have been demonstrated in the creation of mutually beneficial relationships.

Your company may already have a capabilities brochure that covers these points. If your company has a capabilities brochure that covers the majority of these elements, but not all of them, your staff should attempt to utilize the remaining copies, measuring its effectiveness in communication of what your company has now developed as your distinctive capabilities. If the evaluation shows the current version is working adequately, wait until the copies have been used up before developing a new version. If your staff is not satisfied that your distinctive capabilities are being interpreted properly, then your company may want to consider scrapping the old version and going ahead with a new brochure.

Cover Letter The style of this cover letter should be similar to the cover letters written for the awareness action items. The letter should include three succinct messages.

The first message is a summary statement, which should bring the prospective customer up to date on what has occurred so far. A second statement should clearly inform the individual with primary influence what your company's objective is in sending them this capabilities brochure. The statement should show that your staff is trying to provide more information than it did with previous communication materials and is clearly a next step. For example:

> "Over the last few weeks, I have shared with you several pieces of information about our firm. Today, I would like to present a more detailed explanation of our capabilities."

The second message will preview the capabilities brochure. A statement might begin by inviting the individual with primary influence to review the capabilities brochure. A second statement should tell the prospective customer that the brochure will give them a clear idea as to the philosophy, proficiencies, and expertise that makes up your company. Your staff should then extend an invitation to the individual with primary influence to respond should they find that the information within the capabilities brochure is of interest. As with earlier action items, your staff should not expect a response. That is not their objective at this time. However, there will be instances where the timing is perfect, and the process can make significant strides. The final statement in this message should inform the individual with primary influence that in a few weeks your staff will be communicating directly with them to determine the level of interest and to detail their company's needs and service requirements. The tone of this statement should convey that your company's intention is to explore opportunities where there is a match that will benefit both companies. For instance:

> "Enclosed is our company's capabilities' brochure. I would like to invite you to review the brochure at your convenience. Please note any area of interest, and I'd be happy to discuss them with you. I will give you a call in the next few weeks to determine your level of interest in the information I've sent you."

The third message is a positioning statement. This commonly will include the challenges facing your industry and, without naming competitors, how your company has overcome these obstacles and how this may be of value to the prospective customer. Close this message by expressing your company's hopes that this information will be beneficial to the fulfillment of their needs and service requirements for services or products. An example of this third message might read:

"Many companies in our industries face the challenge of increasing the level of service while reducing prices. Many can't compete in this environment. Our company has built a reputation for consistently providing the best value in the industry. I hope the information you read will show how our service can be a benefit to you and your company's success."

Major Capabilities Brochure The five main elements that must be covered in a capabilities brochure are description of the company, service or product capabilities, details of customer service, philosophy of doing business, and quality policy. These five elements come directly from your company's distinctive capabilities.

Some brochures weave these elements through a story of the company's history. Others use bold photos of people and products to illustrate the tone of the company's corporate culture. Still others will pull from a range of elements such as graphs, illustrations, customer quotations, product shots, and imaginative photographs—combining them with the text to relay the story in a conceptual approach. What works best for your company will depend on the criteria your staff develops to serve your company's particular situation.

The first element of the capabilities brochure is a description of the company. This should include a statement that says what industry segment your company is a part of. Another statement should discuss the structure of your company. This might state whether your company is part of a larger corporation, is privately held, publicly traded, or is part of a strategic business alliance that might be relevant to concerns of a prospective customer. A statement should be included that describes geographic characteristics that define your company. Is your company a regional, national, or worldwide provider? The final statement should clearly state the major features that distinguish your company from competitors in your industry.

The second element of the brochure is a description of your service or product capabilities. This will begin with a statement defining the needs and service requirements necessary for a service or product to be successful in your industry. The next statement will build on the needs and service requirements, detailing how your company's service or product have been applied in a flexible manner to develop unique solutions. The next statement should portray the characteristics that define your ideal customers. Who are the customers that your service or product is aimed toward?

The third element of the capabilities brochure details your company's customer service distinction. A statement about the action plans that your company has developed to deliver customer service should be explained. This will include how your staff is able to alter these action plans, offering the flexibility necessary to meet particular customer's needs and service requirements. The next statement summarizes the management structure that facilitates the customer service focus. This may include an overview of procedures followed when there is a service or product failure. A final statement should show the technology your company has utilized to accomplish your company's customer service distinction. Technology may have been utilized to give customers easy access to information regarding order placement, estimating of inventory needs, tracking order fulfillment, estimating delivery dates, or providing information on billing and accounting.

The fourth element of the capabilities brochure to consider is your company's philosophy of doing business. Because your company has decided to follow the Business Development Process, your first statement will include your company's goal of developing mutually beneficial, long-term relationships. A statement should then follow that defines the focus of your company's philosophy. This might explain that your company has committed itself to being the low-cost operator in the industry. It might spell out the value-added emphasis your company has developed in carrying out business activity. Or it may illustrate that your company has invested significantly in developing technology to be the leading service or product innovator in your industry. A statement should also describe the role that training plays in your company's philosophy. This may include a broad spectrum of training, from customer service representatives to management, from safety to total quality management. The last statement that may be prudent to include is the financial philosophy of your corporation. With the changing economic environment that every company has witnessed over the past several years, stability is a major area of importance to prospective customers.

The last element that needs to be included in your company's brochure is a quality policy. Total quality management (TQM) demands that your company meets the expectations of internal and external customers. The first statement in this section should detail what programs your company has established to meet these needs. The second statement should describe your company's commitment to continuous improvement. While your company's service or product meets the current needs and service requirements of your target market, those needs and service requirements are constantly evolving. The next decade will certainly bring an ever-increasing pressure on every company's margins. Your customers and prospective customers will look to your company to improve your services or products and methods of operation as ways of contributing to their own efficiency. Figure 15–1 illustrates the possible layout of a major capabilities brochure and cover letter.

Data Sheets Detailing Specific Service or Product/Cover Letter

The next action will further develop the knowledge the prospective customer has already gained from the capabilities brochure. The purpose of the data sheets is to give the individual with primary influence materials that detail the specific services or products your company provides. This information should be selected by your staff, taking into consideration the prospective customer's needs and service requirements that the staff has gathered to date. The cover letter that accompanies the data sheets needs to assure the individual with primary influence that the services or products describe how your company meet their needs and service requirements.

Figure 15-1 Major Capabilities Brochure/Cover Letter

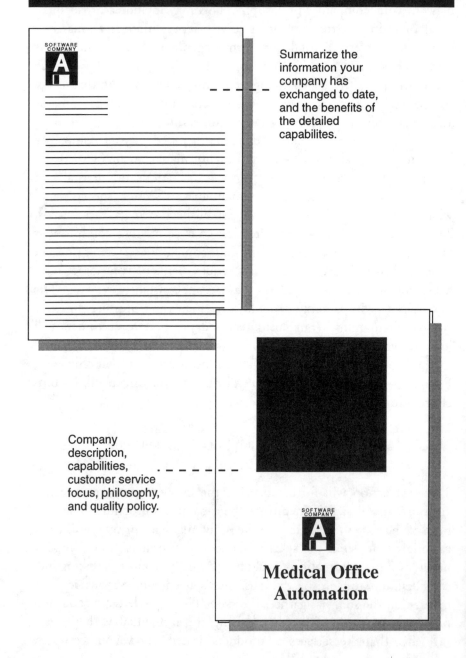

Summarize the information your company has exchanged to date, and the benefits of the detailed capabilites.

Company description, capabilities, customer service focus, philosophy, and quality policy.

Medical Office Automation

Data sheets are different from the general service or product description that were sent to the prospective customer as part of the Awareness step. Data sheets will specifically describe the features of your company's service or product. Where the general service or product description added to the prospective customer's frame of reference, the data sheet will deal in depth with the customer benefits that can be derived.

Cover Letter This cover letter will convey three messages, which should not replicate those in the letter that accompanied the capabilities brochure.

The first message relays your purpose. It first makes a statement that builds continuity by stating that the enclosed material is in support of the information presented in the capabilities brochure. A second statement specifically says why your staff feels the information on the data sheets is important for the prospective customer to understand.

The next message will outline several of the features presented in the data sheets. Then a statement should relate the benefits to the prospective customer's needs. Your staff should state these benefits as characteristics your company has established from working with other customers in their industry.

The final message should reinforce your company's experience. Your staff should develop a statement that is a testimonial of how the features of your company's service or product has benefited your customers. Then a final statement will close the letter with an invitation to contact your company if more specifics are necessary.

Data Sheets Detailing Service or Product The data sheets can take one of several formats. If your company does not already have data sheets that can fulfill this function, the actual form your staff chooses will be dictated by your company's service or product features.

> **Narrative format** This type of data sheet relies on a bold headline statement that describes the customer advantages the service or product provides. Following this headline statement, back-up material, usually in bulleted form, supports the premise. The back-up material should be composed of statistical data that has been collected during the use of the

service or product, or can be detailed service or product specifications.

Features and benefits format This usually takes the form of two columns, one headed Features, the other headed Benefits. Under each heading is a listing in bold text. In normal weight text, a description follows each listing.

Visual format This style uses a photo or illustration of the service or product as the major element. Overprinting the photo or illustration are letter or number notations. Below the photo or illustration, each notation describes the detailed feature and subsequent benefit of each element that is represented.

Any of these formats can serve the function of providing detailed knowledge of your company's service or product. The important measure is determined by which format best complements the distinctive capabilities your company's capability brochure presented, while defining a greater understanding of the service or product. A possible format is shown in Figure 15–2.

Value-Added Suggestion Booklet

Up to this point in the Business Development Process, all materials that you have sent the prospective customer have been informative by nature. That is, they told a story about who your company is, and what your capabilities are, and they provided information about the specific features and benefits of your service or product.

The value-added suggestion booklet is very different by nature. Its purpose is to help the prospective customer, even without their company having purchased your company's service or product. The contents of the booklet will give the prospective customer something of value that the individual with primary influence can use to evaluate, structure, or implement processes that involve your service or product.

By sharing this type of material with the prospective customer, your staff is making a statement about how your company conducts business, competes for business, and expects to be evaluated when procuring new customers. In effect, if the contents of the booklet is

Figure 15–2 Data Sheets Detailing Specific Service or Product/Cover Letter

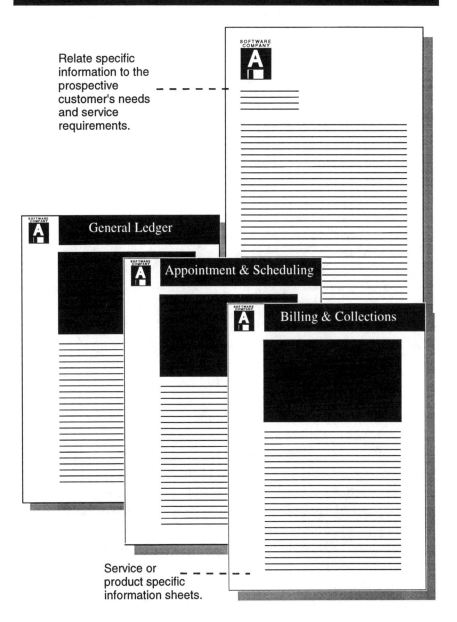

Relate specific information to the prospective customer's needs and service requirements.

General Ledger

Appointment & Scheduling

Billing & Collections

Service or product specific information sheets.

truly valuable from the prospective customer's perspective, it should help the individual with primary influence do his or her job, and at the same time show him or her how your company can deliver a value-added benefit.

The information necessary to create the contents of this value-added suggestion booklet is probably readily available to your marketing and sales staff. The best place to start is to assemble a collection of proposals your staff has developed, prospects' requests for proposals, and customer evaluation surveys. From this collection, an analysis should be developed to determine the type of information that would be of value to the prospective customer. There are three types of value-added suggestion booklet:

➲ How to develop a request for proposal

➲ Service or product development,

➲ Service or product implementation process

How to Develop a Request for Proposal Booklet This type of booklet will give the prospective customer a step-by-step guide to preparing a thorough proposal from service or product providers. This is perhaps the easiest approach for your staff to develop.

The elements that will make up the service or product should be synthesized from requests for proposal your marketing and sales staff have received in the past.

An overview of the booklet should include questions and information requests that are necessary to adequately build a proposal of substantive content. Each question or information request should be supported by information that would be helpful to the prospective customer, either in developing questions in their own request for proposal or in the evaluation of the potential suppliers' response.

It may be tempting to slant the type of questions and information in the booklet to be in the best interest of your company's service or product. However, the booklet will give the greatest impression and have the most benefit to the prospective customer if it is as impartial and unbiased as possible. An example of Printing Company B's approach to this booklet might include information about developing specifications for a bid to print an annual report. This would include a step-by-step guide to determining the length of the document in pages, considering on how different layouts will affect the cost of production, determining how to use color photos to be cost effective while maintaining the highest quality reproduction, and choosing the paper stock to print on and the effect the paper will have on the final piece. The objective of the book would be to give the prospective customer a tool they could use when producing an annual report that will give them all the right questions to ask from whomever they choose to solicit print bids.

Service or Product Development Booklet This booklet will provide the prospective customer with a detailed description of what goes into the development of the service or product your company's industry produces. In other words, this should be an objective look at how any company that provides the service or product fulfills the requirements of the industry.

Your marketing and sales staff will need to bring this process information together by observing the actions that your company takes in developing the service or product. This will include all actions from research and development through delivery. If post-delivery service or training is part of your company's service, that should also be included in the booklet. It is a good idea to research trade publications from your industry to gain a complete understanding of how other companies in your industry fulfill customer requirements. Incorporating these practices with the process your staff produces will make the booklet as objective as possible.

Overall, the booklet should contain sections that sufficiently tell the story behind the service or product. This information will give a first-time user an education equivalent to someone who has worked in the industry for years. For the experienced user, this material will either broaden their perspective, inform them with new developments, or keep them current with issues of concern to the industry. Think of the booklet as a method to make anyone feel like an expert on the service or product.

Again, avoid the temptation to slant this information to the benefit of your company's service or product. Your staff's objective should be to give the prospective customer something of real value. Cellular Service Provider C, for example, could produce a booklet that tells the story of how cellular service was developed. This booklet would include details of the components that go into providing a mobile communications network. Specific topics would include how transmission of the signal takes place between the origin caller, between cells, and routing to the destination caller. New technology such as digital networks would be described along with the advantages this technology delivers. In addition, there would be information on what a virtual office is, and how cellular equipment can be combined with computers, faxes, and electronic data interchanges. With a complete understanding of the components that make up cellular service, the recipient of this booklet will feel like an expert on the subject. And an educated prospect is much more likely to see how your differentiated capabilities will meet their needs and service requirements.

Service or Product Implementation Process Booklet Another kind of booklet provides the prospective customer with a detailed exercise on how to implement a quality process around the service or product that your company's industry provides. This booklet will include detailed instruction on how to define and evaluate the prospective customer's current process that involves the service or product your company produces.

To create this material, your company's staff will clearly detail every action step that is necessary for a process that meets the customer's needs and service requirements. In addition, all action steps that lead up to the process and come out of the process should be documented. If your company already has a total quality management (TQM) system or ISO 9000 program in place, this process will more than likely be documented. If this has not been done or your company has not implemented a process approach to defining action steps necessary in the fulfillment of customer requirements, then the development of this booklet will be extremely beneficial to your company as well.

As a whole, the booklet should give an overview of the advantages, necessary elements, and management needs of a process approach to conducting the action steps necessary in implementing the service or product. This is the most comprehensive approach for the prospective customer in understanding capabilities, specifying requirements, evaluating features, and managing performance.

The booklet should cover the following six topics: First, an introduction needs to demonstrate an understanding of the prospective customer's purchasing situation. This should include the major factors the prospective customer must consider when doing business. Second, it is necessary to define why a structured process is advantageous to the prospective customer. The scope of this topic needs to cover finding and maintaining the best overall value during the life of the service or product. Third, a section needs to cover the issues and options available from the industry that provides the service or product. These issues and options need to be of significant importance to the prospective customer. Fourth, the booklet should include information on how to determine and communicate the prospective customer's needs and service requirements. This section needs to include a list and description of the critical factors that will determine service or product selection as well as vendor selection. Critical buying factors will include performance record, reputation, availability, service network, scope of service or product, cost factors, instruction and training, specialized service or product, payment terms, size of organization (advantages and disadvantages), automated services, and financial stability of service or product provider. Fifth, there should be a section that contains an interactive process to assist the prospective customer in determining of needs and service requirements, judging vendor options, and evaluating proposals. Sixth, a section on a process for vendor management should detail how the prospective customer can maximize fulfillment of needs and service requirements. This topic is an illustration of the entire process. The section needs to include review of needs and service requirements, planning the bidding process, presentation forum, evaluation, vendor designation, service or product execution, performance assessment, and review.

An example for Software Company C might be a booklet that first details all the challenges that face an administrative staff of a medical clinic. The booklet then would use several examples to demonstrate the benefits of a step-by-step process approach to choosing a software vendor that will meet current and anticipated needs and service requirements. The medical software company would also include a section discussing what customers may expect to see in the near future from the medical software applications industry. Next, several worksheets would be included with explanations that would help the prospective customer determineits objectives in automating iys clinic's administration. Additional exercises would allow the prospect to determine a list of needs and service requirements, critical buying factors, and a method for evaluating possible software vendors. The final section of the booklet would be a workshop on how to manage a relationship with a software vendor. This would include tips on how to monitor and measure service, overcome problems, and calculate time savings.

Of all three suggested booklets, the service or product implementation process booklet can be the most valuable to the prospective customer. If your staff has developed objective and relevant material, it demonstrates to the individual with primary influence a real exchange of valuable information that will benefit the prospective customer regardless of vendor selection. A possible layout for a value-added suggestion booklet is illustrated in Figure 15–3.

SUMMARY

In summary, the purpose of the Knowledge step of the Business Development Process is to build service or product knowledge based specifically on the prospective customer's requirements by communicating more detailed information about your company's distinctive capabilities. The communication materials first present a detailed distinctive capabilities picture, then go further into depth relevant to the prospective customer's service or product needs, and finally provide the prospective customer with beneficial user information. These three types of information help give the individual with primary influence the necessary information needed to then continue the two-way education process in the next step. With the prospective customer having gained knowledge of your company's service or product capabilities, the next step of the Business Development Process will educate your company's staff about the prospective customer's needs and service requirements.

FIGURE 15-3   Value-Added Suggestion Booklets

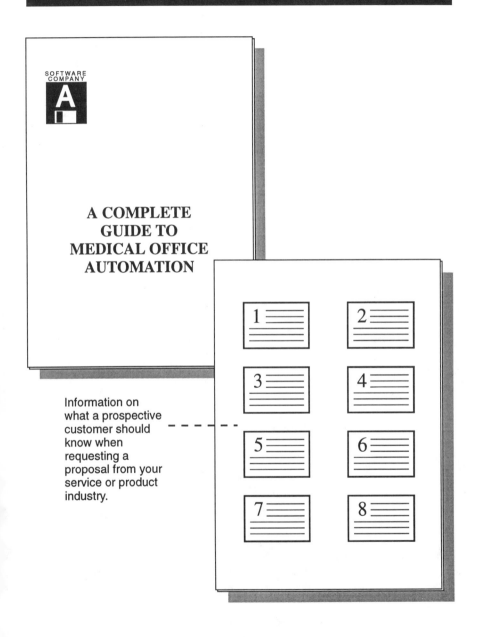

Business Development Process
Step 8: Assessment

The last two chapters have concentrated on educating the prospective customer about your distinctive capabilities. In this chapter, we will again set up a situation that will further your company's education of the prospective customer's requirements. By phone or in person, you will find out perceptions and identify strategic business opportunities. Both your prospective customer and your company now have a basic understanding of how each others' company fits or fails to fit. Your objective is to determine the prospective customer's specific needs and service requirements, so your company can produce an even tighter fit.

Reviewing Information Exchanged to Date

Before your staff begins to further develop your company's education about the prospective customer, preparations need to be made that will make your staff's efforts as productive as possible. Over the course of the past eight to ten weeks, your company has been in contact with the individual with primary influence. During that period of time, different types of information have been exchanged. Most of that information has been developed by your staff and presented to the prospective customer. Some of the communication materials have been general pieces about your company. Other items were specific to the prospective customer because of information your staff received from the individual with primary influence. This information gave your staff some insight into the needs and service requirements of the prospective customer.

Now the Knowledge step of the Business Development Process is complete. The prospective customer has given your company some ideas of what their particular needs and service requirements are. The individual with primary influence also should now have a firm background established with regard to your company's distinctive capabilities, the features and benefits of your company's service or product, and the issues and options available from the industry.

To begin, your staff will need to review prequalification information, review information sent to the prospective customer, and determine possible prospective customer needs and service requirements from preliminary information.

Review Prequalification Information

To begin this process, your staff should review the prequalification information obtained from the survey before the strategic communication plan was begun. The eight topics that were surveyed earlier are as follows: confirmation of service or product usage, type and description of the service or product used, definition of how the service or product is used, who has been supplying the service or product, criteria for selecting competition, evaluation of how well competitors have been fulfilling sales factors, if there is a regular review of service or product, and important features needing attention.

The information you receive from the prequalification survey will vary in the amount of detail. Some prospective customers will have readily provided detailed information. Others will have been more guarded, and will have only given your staff general information. Depending on the depth of the information, your staff has only been able to make certain assumptions about the prospective customers with any accuracy.

From information in the prequalification survey, your staff must determine opportunities for your distinctive capabilities to fit the prospective customer's needs and service requirements. Your staff must understand how the prospective customer incorporated your service or product into its business. The staff also needs to evaluate the critical buying factors the prospective customer uses in determining suppliers. Your staff should also be able to tell how well current suppliers have been meeting the prospective customer's expectations regarding critical buying factors. Finally, your staff will have found out if the opportunity for doing business is immediate, is in the relative near future, or will not present itself for quite some time.

REVIEW INFORMATION SENT TO THE PROSPECTIVE CUSTOMER

The information your staff considered from the prequalification survey influenced what was sent to the prospective customer. The first several items your staff sent should have associated your company's name with its general capabilities. The following items your staff sent should have been more specific to the distinctive capabilities, features, and benefits of your company's service or product. Finally, the information should have further built the prospective customer's knowledge of your industry as a benefit to their company.

Before assessing the prospective customer's needs and service requirements more thoroughly, your staff must first review every item that has been sent. Be sure that every member of the marketing and sales team clearly has a concept of the image your company has been trying to create with communication material in the Awareness and Knowledge steps. Also make sure that all members of the marketing and sales team understand why certain pieces were selected to meet specific needs that the prospective customer revealed in the prequalification survey.

DETERMINE POSSIBLE PROSPECTIVE CUSTOMER NEEDS FROM PRELIMINARY INFORMATION

The success of a sales situation can be greatly enhanced if your marketing and sales staff has been able to uncover a need or service requirement that a current supplier is either not meeting or is not aware of. Your company can be extremely successful if they can use the Business Development Process to identify prospective customers' unfulfilled needs and service requirements, and then to turn those opportunities into new business by offering services or products that meet those specific needs and service requirements. If this did not happen as part of the prequalification survey, it will be the major objective during the Assessment step and the next several steps in the Business Development Process.

The prequalification survey can provide a lot of insight into possible business opportunities. Reviewing how the prospective customer has been using the service or product will disclose whether your company's distinctive capabilities can compete for the business. Reviewing how the prospective customer's needs and service requirements have been met, as well as new needs and requirements that require attention, will open the door to your company as a service or product provider.

The first half of the survey establishes basic customer requirements. Does the prospective customer use the service or product your company offers? What type of service or product has the prospective customer been using? How is the service or product is used? Who has been providing the service?

The second half of the survey reveals how well the current service or product provider is conforming to the prospective customer's requirements. What are the critical sales factors that are used in selecting the service or product provider? Has the current provider been meeting the critical sales factors? Are there important areas that are not being attended to?

DETERMINING PERCEPTIONS

Before your staff can identify possible business opportunities, they will need to determine the prospective customer's perceptions. If there has been no response from the individual with primary influence from the materials that have been presented as part of the Knowledge step, your staff will first want to know how that information has affected their view of your company. As mentioned before, the expectation is not that the prospective customer will respond to the material you have sent. If he or she does respond, your staff is ahead of the game. But the objective is to build the prospective customer's knowledge of your company's distinctive capabilities and service or product.

The individual with primary influence should perceive how his or her company's needs and service requirements fit your company's distinctive capabilities. Your company's capabilities brochure should have communicated your distinctive capabilities clearly to the prospective customer. How did the individual with primary influence perceive those capabilities?

Individual service or product brochures demonstrated your staff's perception of how your company fits with the prospective customer. Does the individual with primary influence share this perception?

The value-added suggestion booklet was intended to give some information of worth to prospective customers and at the same time demonstrate your understanding of the needs and requirements of their industry. Was this demonstrated to the individual with primary influence?

Determining the prospective customer's perception of the communication materials, your service or product, and your company is a major element of the Assessment step. This information will give your staff a great deal of insight into the prospective customer's needs and service requirements. In addition, the perceptions the prospective customer has formulated may very well point the way to identifying business opportunities.

Identify Business Opportunities

Many providers of services and products can promote themselves as having a solution that fits the prospective customer's needs and service requirements. Assessment of the possible business opportunities boils down to two questions: Can the service or product provider live up to the feature and benefit claims it has marketed to the prospective customer? Are there problems for which the prospective customer cannot identify the solutions, but for which your staff can offer unique solutions through the flexible application of your company's service or product?

This means that your staff will need to play interviewer, detective, and troubleshooter as part of the Assessment step, then innovator in developing a solution—the next step of the Business Development Process. In discussions with the individual with primary influence, your staff will need to develop an understanding of the prospective customer's business. In particular, how does the use of your company's service or product affect the prospective customer's ability to add value to their business?

Adding value can be accomplished in one of two ways. First, the function your company's service or product provides will allow the prospective customer to expand its market to more customers. An example for the medical software company would be their prospective customer's ability to be more effective in scheduling, allowing the prospective customer to see more patients. Second, the functions of your service or product allow the prospective customer to lower their costs. For example, the use of the medical software company's product could allow prospective customers to reduce administrative staff and cut those salaries from overhead costs. In either case the use of your company's service or product will lead to margin improvement for the prospective customer.

There may be services and products that provide a function that could be argued neither allows the ability to expand a market nor to reduce costs. These types of services and products could be described as providing some necessary function yet do not add value to the prospective customer's customer. The medical software provides prospective customers with accounting functions that do not add value but are critical to the customer. However, as the economic conditions of this decade and the foreseeable future demanded efficiency and differentiation to remain competitive, services and products must provide value, or they will be eliminated. It is difficult to find an industry whose margins are not being squeezed. Quality management and reengineering are being adopted as survival tactics. Your staff needs to be able to demonstrate the function your service or product provides to their business in terms of the value it adds to the prospective customer. If your staff can uncover such possibilities as part of the Assessment step, the prospective customer will be eager to look at the solutions your staff develops in the next several steps.

Adding value to the prospective customer should be the perspective of your marketing and sales staff in developing an assessment of the business opportunities the prospective customer may present. In some cases, the needs and service requirements that the individual with primary influence presents will be clear. In other cases, your staff may want to thoroughly analyze the prospective customer's business processes that involve your company's service or product.

The Prospective Customer Profile and Assessment Worksheet

The worksheet at the end of this chapter gives your staff a format for profiling the prospective customer and assessing business opportunities. The worksheet is divided into five sections. The first is for the name of the prospective customer, individual with primary influence, phone number, and target industry group. The second section is for a profile of the prospective customer. This might be a paragraph detailing the information known to date, including presurvey information. The third section should be a collection of the communication material that has been presented to the prospective customer up to this point. The last two sections are for recording information obtained in the prospective customer assessment. One paragraph should detail the perception that the individual with primary influence has developed. The other paragraph should contain possible business opportunities that have been uncovered. These may either be requirements that are not being fulfilled by the current service or product supplier, or they may be needs that the prospective customer has not been able to resolve. In either case, your staff's strongest opportunity for fulfilling the business opportunities discovered will be if your solution can offer the prospective customer ways to improve its margin.

This worksheet can be kept as hard copy or as part of an automated network. Regardless of the method, it is a vital tool to be used by your marketing and sales team. Once your company has analyzed the information from the prospective customer, a service or product solutions can be developed. Figure 16–1 is an example of a prospective customer profile and assessment worksheet. On the page that follows, is a blank worksheet (worksheet I) that your company can use.

SUMMARY

The objective of the Assessment step of the Business Development Process is to supplement your staff's education of the prospective customer's needs and service requirements. The outcome of this step will be to identify perceptions and strategic business opportunities. From the strategic business opportunities that have been discovered, your staff can use your service or product to create flexible solutions that further demonstrate the benefits the prospective customer can realize. These benefits are an example of the long-term fit that exists between your company's distinctive capabilities and the prospective customer's needs and service requirements. After the Assessment step of the Business Development Process is complete, your company's marketing and sales staff can begin to demonstrate proof that your company can live up to the service or product expectation you created for conforming to the prospective customer's needs and service requirements.

Prospective Customer Prequalification Survey

Prospective customer: Eastside Medical Clinic   **Date:** 10/15/94
Contact name: Jane Smith - Office Manager   **Phone:** (303)121-0101
Industry: Medical specialty - Sports medicine

Profile
Review prequalification information:

The Clinic is looking for a software solution to automate administration of their office. They are currently using different software for each administrative task: accounting, scheduling, and billing. They want to replace the current software with an integrated package that will result in less time spent on administration. Current software is off the shelf applications adapted to medical needs. Criteria for buying appears to be total time saved in daily operations. Current provider has no medical application background. Currently in review process.

Review sent to prospective customer:

1) Introductory letter, brochure   4) Direct mailer
2) Article reprint   5) Capabilities Brochure
3) Product sheets   6) "Office Automation" booklet

Assessment
Determine possible needs from preliminary information:

The clinic is under staffed. They have a growing number of patients. Account receivables are not up to date. They are in need of automated methods to decrease the amount of manual time required to administer the office.

Determine perception:

The office manager seems to be impressed with the features and benefits of the product. She was very interested after reading the article reprint, because of the comparison of time savings between a manual and automated system.

Identify business opportunities:

There is an immediate opportunity to automate the clinic. If we can prove that time will be saved through the integration of administrative tasks, we have a good chance of gaining the business.

Prospective Customer Prequalification Survey

Prospective customer: _____ **Date:** _____
Contact name: _____ **Phone:** _____
Industry: _____ **FAX:** _____

Profile
Review prequalification information:

_____
_____
_____
_____
_____
_____
_____

Review information sent to prospective customer:

1) _____ 4) _____
2) _____ 5) _____
3) _____ 6) _____

Assessment
Determine possible needs from preliminary information:

_____
_____
_____
_____
_____

Determine perception:

_____
_____
_____
_____
_____

Identify business opportunities:

_____
_____
_____
_____
_____

Business Development Process
Step 9: Proof

This chapter will explain how to develop information that meets the strategic fit determined in the last chapter. Your objective, preliminary to a formal proposal, is to offer proof that your company's distinctive capabilities meet your prospect customers requirements.

Developing Proof Materials

Based on the prospective customer's needs and service requirements and the business opportunities that were determined in the Assessment step, your staff needs to develop material that demonstrates that your company's distinctive capabilities fit their needs and service requirements. The proof materials could be a service or product demonstration, or a testimonial from a current customer that highlights a similar solution your company produced. Another type of proof is a simulation of a possible service or product solution your staff has developed for this particular prospective customer. Finally, your staff could choose to give the individual with primary influence a tour of your company's facilities, if that is an appropriate demonstration of how your company can fulfill the prospective customer's needs and service requirements.

Service or Product Demonstration

One of the most effective demonstrations of proof is to actually show your company's service or product to the prospective customer. Depending on the actual type of service or product, this could take place at the prospective customer's office or at your staff's location.

In most situations, one or more of your staff will be present to perform the demonstration. Be cautious not to use more staff members than are necessary. It is easy to overwhelm the individual with primary influence with too many representatives. The medical software company could set up a demonstration where a few members of their marketing and sales team show how the different components of their integrated office administration product can make a clinic more efficient and reduce administration time.

Some products or services allow for the prospective customer to conduct a demonstration themselves. While many companies feel that they lose a certain amount of control by not having staff present at demonstrations, these demonstrations are often the most effective. The prospective customer is under the least amount of pressure, and if the individual with primary influence is really intrigued, he or she can share the demonstration with other company employees at their leisure. Again, the medical software company might provide a self-running demonstration on disk for prospective customers to use on their own time.

Customer Testimonials

Another effective means of demonstrating proof is customer testimonials. This type of proof material can take a variety of forms. Whatever form your staff develops, the testimonial should directly relate to the prospective customer's needs and service requirements. In other words, if the prospective customer reads a testimonial that says your company is great at performing a type of service, but that is not a type of service that is important to the prospective customer, the testimonial will have little real influence. Testimonials need to have substance behind them if they are to have any power over the prospective customer.

A little creativity in the presentation of the testimonial can greatly enhance the effect. Your marketing and sales staff can use each endorsement to support specific distinctive capabilities, features, or benefits of your company's service or product. The information needs to lead a prospective customer to a conclusion that supports the fit between the two companies. A third-party endorsement offers the most credible evidence that your company can benefit the prospective customer.

The testimonial can demonstrate proof in one of several ways. A portfolio can contain several elements. One could be an opening message from a marketing or sales manager that states their belief that your company can meet the needs and service requirements of the prospective customer. The marketing or sales manager should support his or her statement with particular reasons. A second element in the portfolio should be a chart or graph supporting the message from the marketing or sales manager. A chart or graph that shows a history of the service's or product's performance would be a good example of supporting information for a marketing or sales manager's claim that the service or product is reliable. A third element of the portfolio could be a copy of an endorsement letter from a satisfied customer. Again, this endorsement should be relevant to the claims that the marketing or sales manager is making. The final element to the portfolio might be either a photo or illustration of the service or product, or it could be a diagram that illustrates how the service or product fits into the processes that made it effective for the company offering the testimonial.

A less dramatic approach can be accomplished over time. Whenever your staff receives a testimonial letter, your marketing and sales staff can file it in a library. The letters can be organized by feature, benefit, or element of distinctive capability that is being endorsed. A one-page proof statement can also be created. This proof statement would include a reduction of the testimonial letter, with several key points highlighted. Additional text can be added to support the endorsement. The additional text would go into greater detail or add supporting statistics about the service or product. Figure 17–1 shows what a sample testimonial portfolio might look like.

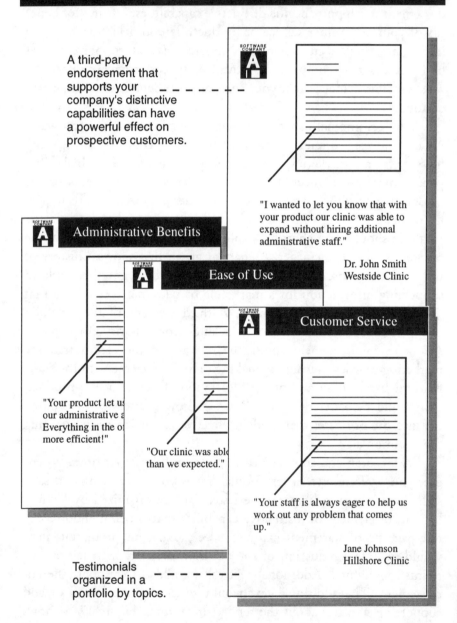

FIGURE 17-1   SAMPLE TESTIMONIAL PORTFOLIO AND ONE-PAGE PROOF STATEMENT

A third-party endorsement that supports your company's distinctive capabilities can have a powerful effect on prospective customers.

"I wanted to let you know that with your product our clinic was able to expand without hiring additional administrative staff."

Dr. John Smith
Westside Clinic

Administrative Benefits

Ease of Use

Customer Service

"Your product let us our administrative a Everything in the o more efficient!"

"Our clinic was able than we expected."

"Your staff is always eager to help us work out any problem that comes up."

Jane Johnson
Hillshore Clinic

Testimonials organized in a portfolio by topics.

Service or Product Simulation

As opposed to a service or product demonstration, a service or product simulation displays an example of the possible prototype solution your staff has created to meet the business opportunity discovered in the Assessment step. This may be the most persuasive of all the forms of demonstrating proof.

The service or product simulation can be particularly useful if the concept behind your company's solution is unique or different. It allows the prospective customer to see not only a possible solution that your staff can offer, but how your staff approaches a situation. This can be one of the major benefits of this type of proof demonstration, regardless of the solution's exact conformance to the prospective customer's needs and service requirements. The important factor is that the approach simulates a substantive solution to the prospective customer's situation. For example, the cellular service provider could set up a simulation for a prospective customer demonstrating a virtual office for field sales using a cellular network and laptop computers. Actual cellular phones, laptops, and software would be set up to simulate how the salesforce would be linked to the home office's electronic mail, cost data for pricing, file transfers for presentations, and for access to sales management information.

The fact that this approach takes an investment in time and creative effort can actually strengthen the relationship with the prospective customer. At best, a demonstration of the service or product your company offers, can only be a show-and-tell session. A service or product simulation gets the prospective customer involved. It also demonstrates that the two-way educational approach your company has taken as part of the Business Development Process is advantageous to both parties.

Your company will stand a much greater chance of success in developing long-term customers if the potential customer believes that your company's distinctive capabilities, services, or products are of real benefit. This will be especially true if your staff has included the expected results your solution will have in terms of increasing the efficiency of the prospective customer's work process—either by decreasing overhead costs or increasing revenue opportunities.

The service or product simulation can be presented in one of several forms. The actual form your marketing and sales staff determines to be the most effective will depend on your company's service or product and the configuration of your staff's solution. When constructing your simulation, remember this is only a simulation, not a proposal. Present enough to intrigue the individual with primary influence, but don't give it all away. Your marketing and sales staff's objective is to demonstrate proof.

Written Simulation The simulation can be done in a written format. This will depend largely on a narrative description of how the solution is applied. First, describe the current situation. This should not be a regurgitation of the obvious, but a confirmation that your staff has a clear understanding of the prospective customer's perspective. Next, provide an overview of the elements that make up your company's service or product solution. This may involve anything from the application of computer technology to on-site product testing. A possible scenario of your company's service or product being applied by the prospective customer should then be described in detail. This fictional account should use factual documentation of your service or product's performance capabilities. For example, if the service or product can shorten the prospective customer's assembly cycle, use statistical examples in the contrived account of its application. You could use information gathered from other customers that detail how their particular assembly cycles were shortened, then build a scenario with information about your prospective customer. Finally, summarize the benefits the prospective customer will realize from your staff's solution.

Audio/Visual Simulation Audio/visual presentation is another effective technique. The difference between the written presentation and an audio/visual presentation will be the use of illustration, animation, and sound. A single or multiple slide show with sound integrated into the presentation can create a more sophisticated atmosphere. A video presentation is another alternative. With the advent of desktop video, your staff can create a simulation on video-tape in-house, at a reasonable cost.

Typically the audio/visual simulation will cover most of the same contents as the written presentation. An introduction will review the prospective customer's situation. Next, key obstacles that your staff's solution will overcome need to be identified. Instead of a written narrative, the scenario will be demonstrated using visuals, with titles or a voice-over to lead the individual with primary influence through the idea. As in the written presentation, facts about the performance or features of your company's service or product will be used to tell a fictional account of the solution your staff has developed. The final element should be a summary of the benefits that the prospective customer will recognize.

Model Simulation Another form of simulation is a model that demonstrates the service applications or product functions. Depending on the type of service or product your company produces and the ideas your staff needs to indicate, the complexity of the model will vary. For example, if your company produces any type of equipment, a model could prototype the solution by simulating display readouts, performance cycles, and machinery movements.

In any case, the model should be a three-dimensional representation of the solution that will meet the needs and service requirements of the prospective customer. The effectiveness of this approach is dependent both on the interactiveness of the demonstration and the success of communicating a unique solution.

Products naturally lend themselves to demonstrations in the form of models. However, many services can be effectively illustrated by using three-dimensional models as well. If in the judgment of your staff, the prospective customer needs this type of approach to understand the solution, this may be the better approach.

A model that demonstrates proof of your company's solution needs to be supported by a presentation. In most cases, this will be an in-person presentation by a member of your marketing or sales team. A script should be constructed in advance that analyzes the current situation, the premise used to develop this solution, and how the model of the solution works, and then summarizes the gains the prospective customer will recognize from the solution.

Computer Simulation This last solution utilizes technology that is now readily available. Software is now available to automate the process of presenting a conceptual solution. The advantages of using a computer to present ideas to the prospective customer comes both from the multimedia capabilities and the interactive features of this kind of demonstration. Animation, moving pictures, illustration, voice, and interactive participation can be programmed for a consistent presentation.

A simulation of a solution as a form of demonstrating proof has its risks as well as its rewards. Your company has no assurance that the time and energy your staff invests into your solution will pay dividends. In fact, there is no assurance that the prospective customer won't take the solution your company proposes and have it implemented by their current service or product provider. Since your company has provided this solution as a way of demonstrating proof that there is a fit between your company's distinctive capabilities and the prospective customer's needs and service requirements, your staff cannot ask for compensation for your company's time.

The rewards, on the other hand, can be great. A prospective customer may feel that the solution, even if it's not the exact answer, offers so much possibility he or she may they ask for a proposal. In many cases, the exercise will give the individual with primary influence enough of an experience working with your staff that he or she will then have a sample of what it would be like to have your company as a service or product provider. In many cases, this approach is the best way to demonstrate the benefits that the prospective customer will gain when it enters into a business relationship with your company.

FACILITY TOUR

Another means of demonstrating proof to the prospective customer is a guided tour of your company's facilities. This is an appropriate form if a major component of your company's distinctive capabilities is dependent on the plant, office, or staff. To many individuals with primary influence, seeing the actual facility where the service or product is generated is the proof behind all the claims that have been made in your company's communication materials.

Another important benefit of a facility tour is that it allows the prospective customer the ability to broaden the relationship with your staff. To date, the prospective customer may have spoken to a few members of your marketing and sales staff and possibly met one or two of them in person. The tour provides them with the opportunity to speak with the staff members who will actually perform the tasks involved in delivering the service or producing the product. The people behind the scenes may be one of your company's greatest assets in marketing your company.

Seeing the actual plant or office can differentiate your company from the competition. Actually seeing the technology that is used to maintain a service, or the equipment that manufactures the product, allows the individual with primary influence to become involved with your company. This involvement is an important ingredient in establishing a relationship that makes both parties partners in a process that creates a win-win business situation.

Summary

The Proof step of the Business Development Process provides your staff with the objective of demonstrating proof that your company can conform to the needs and service requirements of the prospective customer. This step allows the individual with primary influence to learn how your staff can apply flexible solutions using your company's service or product to create beneficial resolutions to strategic business opportunities. With a demonstration of proof that your company's distinctive capabilities meet the prospective customer's needs and service requirements, your company will be in position to develop a strategy that will close the sale with a formal proposal.

Part V

A Tactical Plan
and Solution

Business Development Process
Step 10: Strategy

Part IV explained how to further expand your company's level of understanding of the prospective customer's needs and service requirements and the prospective customer's understanding of your company's distinctive capabilities. This section will focus on developing a tactical plan to gain the prospective customer's business and tailoring a proposal to exactly meet the prospective customer's needs and service requirements. If the earlier process of two-way communication has been successful, these two steps will be relatively easy.

Up to this point, the Business Development Process has been a two-way exchange of information. This exchange has raised both the prospective customer's knowledge of your company's distinctive capabilities and your staff's knowledge of the prospective customer's needs and service requirements. The result should create a shared understanding of the fit that exists between the two companies and the possibilities of a mutually beneficial, long-term business relationship.

The development of a tactical plan to gain the prospective customer's business is the next step of the Business Development Process. It is at this point that the objective changes from informational exchanges designed to build a relationship to a sales objective designed to produce the commitment to do business. Your staff will now form a team that can analyze the information and situation and determine a strategy to accomplish this commitment. If your company is a small business, your strategy team may be made up of only a few staff members who share multiple responsibilities. A larger company may have a team made up of groups of two to five members.

The strategy needs to be comprehensive in order to incorporate every aspect of your company in delivering your service or product solution. This means that the strategy team needs to be composed of groups representing the different issues and concerns from multiple areas of your company including: marketing, sales, administration, research and development, pricing, and customer service.

TEAM-BASED DETERMINATION OF SALES STRATEGY

The team should be organized by the marketing and sales staff who have brought the prospective customer to the Proposal step. The team should also include groups of experts assembled from the different areas of the company, whose skills apply to meeting the needs and service requirements of the prospective customer. These diverse groups that form the team will ensure that the proposal incorporates the internal requirements that different departments may have for supplying the service or product. For example, your marketing and sales staff might not be aware of how possible customer service commitments may be to fulfill. Another example might be a customer's billing request, and how easily your company's accounts receivable department can accommodate the request. This is an important consideration, because by taking into account both the internal and external requirements, the problems that may arise with providing the service or product to a new customer can be avoided. Avoiding start-up problems can be the key to building a long-term business relationship. Figure 18–1 illustrates the concept of team-based determination of sales strategy.

THE MARKETING GROUP

The group members from the marketing department will serve two functions on the strategy team. First, they will be able to offer creative concepts on how service or product features may be structured in a flexible manner to meet the particular prospective customer's situation. This insight comes from the knowledge the marketing department has gained about the particular prospective customer from being a part of

FIGURE 18–1   TEAM-BASED DETERMINATION OF SALES STRATEGY

Strategy Team Composition

the Business Development Process. The nature of the marketing department's work with communicating the distinctive capabilities of the company will have given the group's members a unique view of the company's service or product. In addition, the marketing group should gain even more insight from analysis of the margin potentials of particular services or products in varying usage patterns. From customer surveys, the group should also have a good perception of what solutions and situation have been the most satisfactory to existing customers in similar industries. Competitor intelligence that marketing has collected can also provide insight into the types of solutions other service or product providers may attempt to offer the prospective customer.

The second function of the marketing group will be to actually produce and coordinate the proposal. This will include determining what information will be in the proposal. The marketing group will be responsible for requesting data from other individuals within your company, as well as for obtaining any necessary outside information. Team members from the department will prepare any necessary visuals, charts, and graphs.

The Sales Group

The sales group will play several major roles in the Strategy step of the Business Development Process. Sales brings to the strategic team the closest experience with prospective customers. The experience the sales group has in selling to other customers in the same industry offers a unique perspective of what it will actually take to close the sale with the prospective customer. The sales group can best judge the balance between the price your company will ask for the service or product and the value-added elements that will be formulated into the service or product. Also, the members of the sales group should have a great deal of knowledge about the industry. They must have an understanding of the value that the prospective customer is offering to its own customer; what issues and obstacles face the prospective customer's industry; they should also have a keen awareness of what competitors' salesforces will be offering the prospective customer. The sales group will be relied upon to play the role of devil's advocate when evaluating the proposal's contents.

The sales group's other responsibility will be to present the proposal to the prospective customer. This will require the sales group to have a good grasp of the information and the solutions presented in the proposal. The sales group members need to feel they have the service or product understanding that will enable them to answer any objections that may arise during the proposal presentation to the satisfaction of the prospective customer. The sales group will need to have the necessary skills to make the presentation, and they will need to be able to move the prospective customer to the point where it can produce the commitment to use your company's service or product.

The Customer Service Group

The involvement of a group consisting of customer service staff is also critical. If the prospective customer is to approve your firm as a service or product provider, the customer service group will be out in front of the customer, delivering the service or product that conforms to the customer's needs and service requirements. If the relationship grows into a long-term business relationship, with your company designated a preferred vendor, it will be because your company's customer service group has been able to meet the customer's expectations. As the strategy team develops the process for the proposed solutions, the customer service group must be able to determine if it is possible to consistently deliver the necessary customer service related to the service or product solution. If your company's proposed solution includes a 24-hour 800 phone number for the prospective customer to call in any questions, does your customer service group have staffing for 24-hour assistance?

The Research and Development Group

This group is composed of members whose responsibility is for the actual development of the service or product. Group members must know what is or is not possible to create, in order to meet the prospective customer's needs and service requirements. In producing a strategy for the proposal, the R & D group must use the creative ideas raised by the marketing group, the prospective customer insight presented by the sales group, and the consistent delivery of service or product support determined by the customer service group, to find ways for your company to make the actual solution possible. If a proposed solution can solve a critical area of concern for the prospective customer, but your company is unable to come through with the actual development, a long-term business relationship will never take place. Your R & D group must have a good sense of the scope of what can be produced with the resources available.

The Administration Group

The administration group must also be part of the strategy team. It must be able to meet the prospective customer's performance reporting and billing requirements. In addition, the administration group may need to perform other tasks as part of the strategy team, such as collecting similar data on past customers and providing financial information that may be important to the prospective customer.

The Pricing Group

Group members responsible for pricing must be capable of building a model of the costs of the proposed solution. This should include an assessment of all costs in terms of both staff time and material that will be needed to deliver the service or product. The pricing group will have to then determine the necessary margin return necessary from sales to the prospective customer. If there is an investment in research and development for your company to create the proposed solution, the pricing group needs to determine how long it will take for the return on investment to be realized. Different scenarios may have to be depicted, depending on the type of volume the prospective customer represents, as well as other factors that could be involved in the business relationship. The entire team will need to evaluate the outcome of these scenarios.

Developing a Strategy Process

A strategy process is a series of steps that need to be taken in order to create the service or product solution that your company can then develop into a proposal. The strategy process needs to be developed so that all consequences of your company's solution are thoroughly understood by the team and all problems are resolved. The process that your company's staff uses to develop a strategy to gain the business of the prospective customer should consider both inputs and outputs from both the prospective customer and from within your company.

Inputs to the strategy process are the prospective customer's needs and service requirements, which your staff has determined. Also considered an input into the strategy process are the prospective customer's reaction to the materials that your staff prepared as part of the Proof step. From within your company, the costs of developing and delivering the solution, as well as your company's service or product and distinctive capabilities will also be the inputs to the strategy process. For example, if a prospective customer of Printing Company B has the requirement for a two-week completion schedule, then that becomes an input.

Outputs are how your company's solution meets the prospective customer's needs and service requirements. This will include the price being considered a fair value for the service or product, and the value-added benefits of the service or product. Other outputs from within your company include margin potential, customer service commitments, solution and proposal presentation, research and development time, measurement methods of meeting the customer's requirements, and long-term development of business opportunities with the prospective customer. An example for Printing Company B might be the final price it needs to charge the prospective customer due to rush charges and overtime costs to meet the two-week completion schedule.

By carefully considering all the inputs and outputs to the strategy process, your staff can develop a cohesive, well-thought-out strategy. Between the inputs and outputs will be a step-by-step time line, including all details of the plan. Every action will have been weighed against the input and output requirements to ensure that the proposed solution conforms to all elements, from concept through development and from implementation through administrative issues. Figure 18–2 illustrates one possible outline of a strategy process.

Figure 18–2   Developing a Sales Strategy Process

Strategy Process

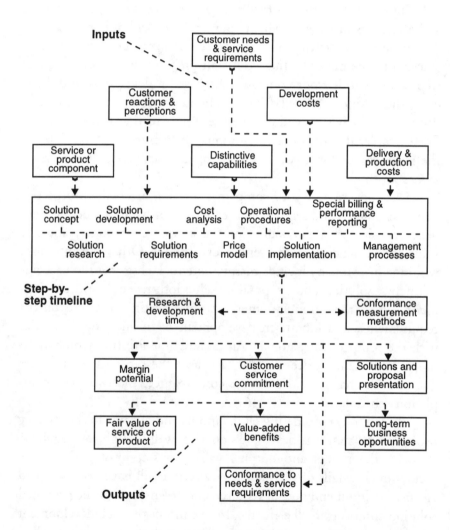

SUMMARY

The objective of the Strategy step of the Business Development Process is to develop a tactical process plan for gaining a commitment from the prospective customer. The process must be comprehensive. Every possible ramification and effect that any element of the solution may cause needs to be considered against the prospective customer's needs and service requirements, as well as your company's requirements. The Strategy step will allow your staff to produce a proposal that will invite a business relationship, offering the prospective customer a service or product that benefits its company by decreasing overhead costs or increasing revenue opportunities. In addition, the result will be a proposal that your company's strategy team has thoroughly examined to bring the maximum potential return to your company from the new business relationship. Now, your company's staff is ready to produce a proposal tailored to exactly meet the prospective customer's needs and service requirements.

Business Development Process
Step 11: Proposal

Once the strategy developed in the last chapter is complete, a tailored sales proposal can be constructed. The objective of the proposal is to introduce the prospective customer to the service or product solution, as well as answer any remaining questions. In addition to presenting the solution your staff has formulated, the proposal must also assist in developing a deeper understanding of your company's history, philosophy, distinctive capabilities, and services or products.

The proposal your company will present to the prospective customer is a visual and written representation of your company's solution. This, without question, is the most critical of any document in the entire Business Development Process. It must bring together all the information that has been exchanged as part of the two-way educational process. But it must also go further. Beyond any earlier communication, the proposal must detail a plan to implement a service or product solution that, from the perspective of the individual with primary influence, clearly demonstrates a measurable benefit to the prospective customer.

Every element of the proposal should be developed from a customer-driven point of view. This is not an easy task. The marketing group and the strategy team have been given the responsibility to produce the proposal and will need to utilize all data and information your company has acquired in putting together your company's solution to meet the prospective customer's specific needs and service requirements. Figure 19–1 illustrates the elements of a tailored sales proposal.

Elements of the Proposal

The proposal consists of six elements: the introduction, the situation analysis, the service or product plan, service or product details, pricing, and answers to anticipated questions and objections.

Introduction to Your Company

The purpose of the first section of the proposal is to present a detailed image of your company. This description goes beyond information that may have been presented in bits and pieces with earlier marketing communication. The proposal should get the prospective customer excited about who your company is, the reputation that it has built, and the future direction it is planning.

The company introduction should tell the story of your company, supported with statistics and facts that are relevant to the prospective customer. The story will make four main points that will gain the confidence of the individual with primary influence. The primary point illustrates that your company is a quality provider of the service or product. The second point is that your company has a history of delivering value to customers. The third point is that your company has been able to accomplish the previous two points while maintaining financial stability. The fourth point presents how your company's process uses technologies to stay in the forefront of your industry in supplying its service or product. The future benefit of these technologies will be fundamental to the prospective customer's use of your company's service or product.

Situation Analysis

The objective of a situation analysis is to clearly state your company's understanding of the environment and circumstances that the prospective customer faces. The detail necessary in this section will depend on

Figure 19–1   Elements of a Tailored Sales Proposal

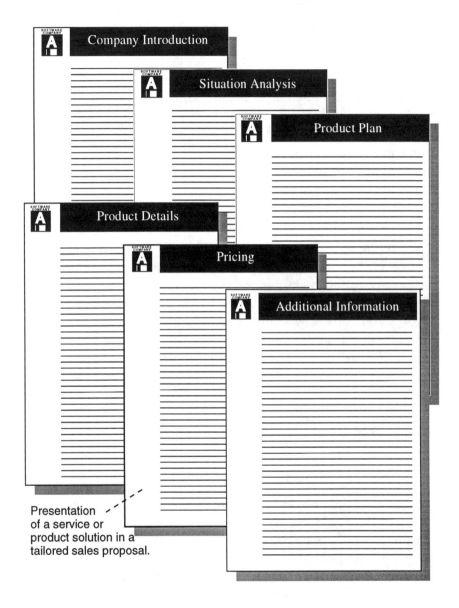

Presentation of a service or product solution in a tailored sales proposal.

your particular service or product and how it interfaces with the needs and service requirements of the prospective customer. In some industries, the situation may be so obvious that it doesn't warrant much detail. For example, Printing Company B has a prospective customer who is producing an annual report. However, in most cases the situation analysis is not only an excellent opportunity to demonstrate that your staff has been listening to the individual with primary influence's needs and service requirements, but it also sets the stage for the solution your staff will present in the next section of the proposal. Printing Company B might write a situation analysis that states an understanding of why last-minute financial statement changes will need to be made in the annual report, as well as a comprehension of the time restraints placed on the prospective customer's staff.

The situation analysis should not simply be a restatement of what the prospective customer has told you. It needs to present a scenario of the challenges your company sees facing both the particular prospective customer and the prospective customer's industry at large. Then it must further analyze what effects these challenges will have on overhead costs as well as revenue opportunities.

The threats and opportunities that face every industry will vary greatly. But the earlier process of determining strategies should have revealed the process your prospective customer involves when using the service or product. This should be the key to demonstrating a deeper understanding from a customer-driven perspective of your prospective customer and its situation.

Service or Product Plan

The service or product plan serves two purposes: to present the solution your staff has developed to the prospective customer's problem and to explain in detail the service or products relevant to the solution your company is proposing.

The presentation of your company's solution will describe in detail the specifics of a plan meeting all the prospective customer's needs and service requirements. The solution should include five major messages.

1. **Overview:** The first message will be a simplified overview of the concept presented in the solution. This should utilize both a narrative and a visual illustration. Different individuals will comprehend a solution in different ways. Using both methods to present the overview will maximize the impact of the solution.

2. **Major elements:** The second message will identify the major elements involved in the solution and explain them in detail. This must include how the application of your service or product will work toward meeting the needs and service requirements of the prospective customer. A process map should be used to detail the major elements of the solution. An effective means of presenting the process map is a bubble diagram, which consists of a box with the title of the action step inside. Between each action step is an arrow that shows the direction of the process flow. Following the diagram is a narrative that explains the action step that each box represents. Figure 19–2 shows an example.

3. **Implementation:** The third message will state how the solution will be implemented. The success of a well-designed solution will depend on a complete and comprehensive implementation. This will include time schedule, start-up costs, and training.

    A time schedule must estimate how much time each of the initial action steps will take to complete, including any work that has to be accomplished before the actual use of the service or product can begin. The following are some areas to consider, depending on the type of service or product:

    ➲ Adapting the prospective customer's current work process.

    ➲ Altering facilities to accommodate the use of the service or product.

    ➲ Administrative tasks such as billing and special service or usage reports

    ➲ Hardware and software compatibility and electronic link-ups.

    ➲ Staff training.

FIGURE 19–2   SOLUTION PROCESS MAP OF MAJOR ELEMENT

Strategy Process

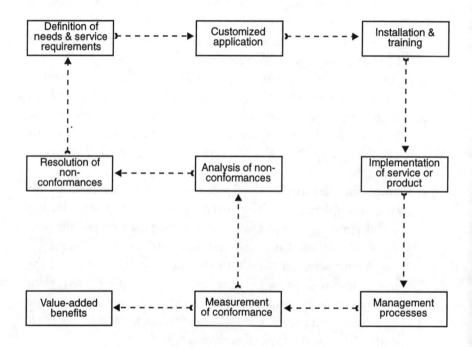

Start-up costs should be approximated as much as possible and should include what preliminary actions need to be accomplished, why the implementation justifies the expense, and who is responsible for paying the expense (the service or product provider, or the prospective customer). Different types of services or products will require different start-up costs, but be sure to consider the following:

➲ Construction costs to modify facilities for service or product use.

➲ Purchasing of hardware and software.

➲ Setting up and maintaining electronic link-ups.

➲ Staff training.

Any training necessary for the service or product to be properly used also needs to be included. Include who is responsible for initiating the training, who will be providing the training, and who will keep records of completed training. (The latter may be required for some service or product use by government agencies.) Possible areas of training that need to be covered include the following:

➲ Application of the service or product.

➲ Safety issues.

➲ Hardware, software, and electronic link-up use.

➲ Work process procedures.

➲ Advanced applications.

4. **Management process:** The fourth message that needs to be discussed is your company's management process; in other words, what mechanics are in place to monitor the effectiveness of your service or product to meet the needs and service requirements of the prospective customer. Your company's management process needs to include measurement of how the needs and service requirements are being met, regular review

and evaluation of the results, and modification of the service or product solution if indicated by the results. In addition, your management process needs to include a formal method for resolving conflicts. This method should include how your company will deal with any foreseeable problems, from customer satisfaction to billing errors.

5. **Benefits:** The last message in this section of the proposal needs to specify list the benefits of the solution. As mentioned earlier, the benefits of your company's proposed solution needs to be customer-driven. Each of the benefits your staff lists needs to add value to the prospective customer's business. The value that is added should clearly affect the prospective customer's costs to either produce or deliver its service or product, allow it to generate more revenue from existing sources, or open up new sources of revenue. If possible, avoid the simple explanation of each benefit your staff feels the prospective customer will realize. Thoroughly review the research your staff developed in formulating the strategy and the solution. From the information your company has gathered about the prospective customer and its industry, provide significant consequences and how those consequences will benefit the prospective customer.

SERVICE OR PRODUCT DETAILS

Following the presentation of your company's solution, the next section of the proposal details the specifications of the service or product. The service or product specification section needs to include a detailed description of the service or product features. A statement of the needs and service requirements the service or product fills should also be included. For example, if you were a manufacturer of exercise equipment, you would want to go into detail about how each feature works: how to adjust the product for different body sizes, how the biofeedback instruments work, etc. Following this description you would list each of the needs and service requirements the prospective customer has specified, and opposite each one detail how the product meets those requirements.

PRICING

Pricing should also be clearly detailed. The way the Business Development Process has been constructed, the prospective customer should have a good sense that the price is justified by the value-added benefits they will realize from your company's solution. To clearly state the value that the prospective customer is going to receive, your staff should clearly specify the costs involved with your company's service or product solution. Following the cost, your company must then justify the expense to the prospective customer, from their perspective. This may not always be easy; however, your staff must put themselves in the prospective customer's place. For instance, the medical software company would list the cost for each module of its integrated software: scheduling, accounts receivable, patient insurance records, etc. Then list the time savings over the prospective customer's current system. Estimating the approximate cost in employee salary, the medical software company can justify the cost of the software by the amount of time necessary to pay back the investment in terms of employee salary savings. Or better yet, observe a situation where your company must purchase a service or product that is required to carry out your business. What makes your staff feel comfortable when justifying the value of a service or product purchase? Realize that the prospective customer is going through the same process. If the prospective customer can feel comfortable with the value it is going to receive for the price your company will charge, you will not have a problem.

ANSWERS TO Additional QUESTIONS and Objections

The final section of the proposal should answer any additional questions or objections that your staff feels the prospective customer is likely to have. While the marketing group is preparing the proposal it is a good opportunity for the sales group to review each section. As they critique the proposal, sales should play the role of devil's advocate. Since the members of the sales group should have the closest contact with the individual with primary influence, they should be better able to anticipate areas of concern that have not been covered elsewhere in the proposal.

SUMMARY

In summary, the objective of the Proposal step is to communicate a clear and precise proposal for your company's solution. The proposal should emphasize a customer-driven perspective that specifically justifies every feature of the service or product solution. Your staff has fulfilled its purpose if the proposal persuades the prospective customer to pay your price for the benefits they believe they will receive from the value-added solution.

PRESENT AND CEMENT

Business Development Process
Step 12: Approval

Part VI will focus on the steps of the Business Development Process that will bring the prospective customer to the center of the bull's-eye target model: closing the sale and establishing a long-term relationship. The objective of the Approval step is to be approved as a vendor, giving the prospective customer evidence of fulfilling commitments made in the proposal. The objective of the Preference step is to cement the relationship with your company as the preference for supplying the service or product.

This chapter will first concentrate on what efforts are needed for your company to be approved as a service or product provider. Then, we will look at a system that, once your company has been approved as a service or product provider, will keep your company in a position to prove its value to the customer.

Over the course of the Business Development Process, your company has moved the prospective customer toward the center of the bull's-eye target model. When the prospective customer was on the outer ring of the target, it had little or no name awareness of your company. As it moved systematically through the different rings, its level of awareness of your company and knowledge of your company's distinctive capabilities grew. Simultaneously, your staff's understanding of the prospective customer's needs and service requirements has grown. As the prospective customer advanced to the center of the target, your staff developed specific solutions to meet its needs and service requirements. The solution has now been developed into a proposal for presentation to the prospective customer.

THE PRESENTATION FORMAT

Now the challenge is for your sales staff to present the proposal to the individual with primary influence and gain a commitment to do business. Many factors will go into the prospective customer's evaluation and eventual decision on using your company as a service or product provider. Some of these factors your company will have little or no control over. But the prospective customer has made it to this stage of the Business Development Process because at each progressive step the fit between your company and theirs has become tighter and tighter. The proposal should be a vision of how the actual business relationship will work. Closing the sale should not be a struggle. It should only come down to working out any small differences in the two companies' perception of the vision.

The format of the presentation can run the spectrum in terms complexity. Whichever method your company chooses should make the prospective customer feel comfortable.

Simple presentation: A simple presentation can involve gathering around the prospective customer's conference table. Your staff should prepare copies of the proposal for all participants. Several members of your staff may be present, but one member of your sales group should be designated to make the actual presentation.

Complex presentation: The other extreme can be an elaborate display with the prospective customer invited to your company's facility. The marketing group could prepare a multimedia presentation that uses slides, video, or computer-generated display to create a simulation of the solution. This type of presentation might involve several of your company's strategy team members to deliver the key parts of the proposal that are relevant to their areas of expertise.

In any case, be certain that the format your staff has chosen for the presentation of the proposal fits the prospective customer. Get a feel for the prospective customer from members of your marketing and sales team who may have had experience with similar types of customers. A presentation that is too fancy may make a prospective customer feel your approach to doing business is too slick. A presentation that is not elaborate enough could make the prospective customer feel that your company does not place enough value on its business.

The Proposal Presentation

The proposal should be presented in a logical sequence that builds a case for the acceptance of your company as the service or product provider. While there are any number of ways a proposal can be presented, the following suggestions give a basic structure to a presentation.

1. Begin with the designated leader of your sales group introducing the members representing your company. Give a brief statement explaining why they have been included in the presentation. For example, you might include a member from the customer service department and one from the product development department. State how their expertise will serve in making your company's solution beneficial to the prospective customer.
2. Give a brief summary of each section of the proposal.
3. Go into the details of each section of the proposal, one section at a time. Be sure to explain all visuals clearly .
4. Conclude each section by asking the representatives of the prospective customers for any questions, objections, or concerns.
5. Respond as necessary, unless the question, objective, or concern will be dealt with later in the presentation. Make that known, and proceed to the next section of the proposal.
6. At the conclusion of the last section of the presentation, summarize the customer benefits. One effective way of doing this is to list the major needs and service requirements that were identified by your company. Next to each one, list how your company's service, product feature, or distinctive capability that

meets the particular need or service requirement. Follow that by listing the value-added benefit the customer will realize from the implementation of the solution. Be sure to have a graphic that represents this summary.

Following the conclusion of the presentation, the prospective customer will need to review the proposal. This may take several days or weeks, depending on the complexity of the solution, other proposals that the prospective customer may be receiving, or its internal approval process. Your company may be called upon to answer further questions or concerns or to work out details of the proposed solution before your company is approved as a service or product provider. The Business Development Process does not guarantee that your company's proposal will be approved. However, if this process has been followed, and the prospective customer has been brought closer and closer into the center of the target, the tight fit and subsequent benefits to both companies should be clear. The effort your company has put forth should be maximized, and the results will give your company the greatest opportunity for success.

Continuous Monitoring of Customer Requirements

Once your company has been approved as a service or product provider, your company must set up a system for continuous monitoring of the customer's needs and service requirements. Regardless of how close both your prospective customer and your staff felt the service or product solution fit, it is impossible to know for sure until the service or product is in use. It is critical to the final steps of the Business Development Process that the solution is monitored and adjusted to be sure that, indeed, the needs and service requirements match the service or product solution.

The Five-Step Monitoring Process

The simplest model to follow is a circular five-step monitoring process, which returns to the first step as soon as the fifth step is completed. The process's five steps are: 1) written statement of customer needs and service requirements, 2) monitoring of customer service or product usage, 3) measurement of fulfillment of needs and service requirements, 4) analysis of fit/misfit model, and 5) adjustment of service or product.

1. **Written statement of customer needs and service requirements:** The process begins immediately when your company initiates service or product by producing a written statement of the customer's needs and service requirements. This is an important communication step both for your company's internal and external customers. Externally, your customer should agree that these written needs and service requirements are what will be measured. Internally, your staff should equally understand that your company has made a commitment to fulfill these exact needs and service requirements.

2. **Monitoring of customer service or product usage:** The second part of the process is monitoring the service or product that is actually used by the customer. This consists of observing the customer applying the product or service in actual circumstances. Monitoring the customer can take place as part of a regular maintenance program or as a conclusion to the training your company provides to customers.

3. **Measurement of needs and service requirements:** The third step is measurement of the needs and service requirements fulfillment. Depending on what the agreed-upon needs and service requirements are, your company will need to formulate some type of quantitative way of measuring whether the service or product solution is meeting expectations. This could be some type of performance measurement. For a service, it might mean measuring performance completed on schedule; for a product, it might mean measuring the number of hours used without a breakdown; for either a service or product, it might mean measuring correct billing.

4. **Analysis of fit/misfit model:** The fourth step should analyze the measurement against the written statement of needs and service requirements, then compare that measurement to the fit/misfit model constructed earlier in the Strategy step to identify areas where a misfit is occurring. For example, the

medical software company has been measuring the hours the customer has been saving against the written needs or service requirement to save 25 percent over the previous administrative system. If the 25 percent is not being met, the fit/misfit model would be used to identify where the misfit is occurring. In this case it may indicate that the application has required a double entry where it was not necessary.

5. **Adjustment of service or product:** The fifth step determines what adjustment needs to be made in the service or product solution. This adjustment only needs to be made if a misfit is identified.

The outcome of the five-step process should always be communication with the customer. Following the fifth step, your staff should begin again at Step 1, reviewing the written statement of customer needs and service requirements. As time proceeds, those needs and service requirements may change, and those changes should be noted in the statement.

Figure 20–1 illustrates the continuous monitoring of customer requirements.

SUMMARY

The first objective of the Approval step of the Business Development Process is to present the solution your company has developed in a proposal format. The second objective is to close the sale and become an approved provider. The third objective is to begin providing a service or product while implementing a process to monitor fulfillment of your company's service or product solution. With this step accomplished, becoming a long-term provider of the service or product is your company's next objective.

Figure 20–1   Continuous Monitoring of Customer Requirements

Five Step Monitoring of Customer Requirements

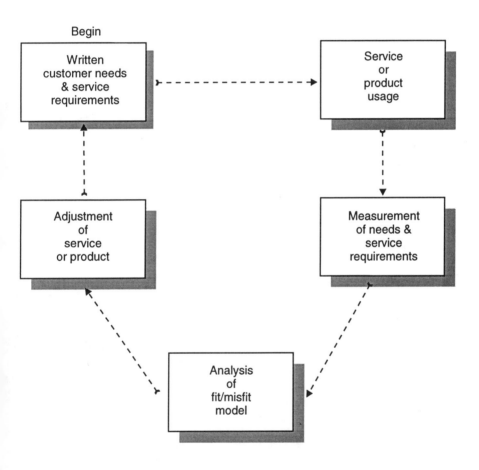

Business Development Process
Step 13: Preference

The final step of the Business Development Process deals with your company's ability to be selected as the preferred provider of the particular service or product. The objective of this chapter is to set up a process to keep the customer's business by continuously providing the quality of service or product that meets the customer's changing expectations.

As an approved provider of a service or product, your company has been given the opportunity to be supplier to the customer. Depending on the type of service or product, your company is probably only one of several approved providers. In most cases, a customer will want to gain some experience working with your company before evaluating future opportunities for working together.

The goal set at the beginning of the Business Development Process was to develop long-term customers. This final step is designed to move the customer to the very center of the bull's-eye target model. Developing your company's relationship from approved provider to preferred provider means developing a proven track record of providing a service or product that is flexible enough to adapt to changes in the customer's needs and service requirements. In addition, the service or product solution must be consistent enough to demonstrate a measurable value-added benefit to the customer's bottom line (i.e., lower overhead costs or new revenue).

To become the preferred provider, your company must first deliver to the customer's satisfaction the service or product that served as your company's proposed solution. Then your staff must develop a process that continues the strategy and solution functions formulated in the original proposal. In other words, your staff must always be looking at the inputs and outputs of the customer's needs and service requirements.

As the business environment that your company and the customer works in changes, your staff will need to respond. The business environment might be affected by technological improvements that affect the service or product you provide to your customer. The business environment could be affected by new competitive factors that affect your customer's business. The business environment might be affected by competitive pressures from a new service or product provider entering your market. The business environment could be affected by social, economic, or political events that affect both companies. Whatever the case, when your company is given the opportunity to provide the service or product, your staff's objective must be to use your company's distinctive capabilities to contribute measurable means for the customer to lower its costs or gain profitable revenue. If this can be accomplished, the transition from approved to preferred provider will not be difficult.

INSTITUTING A CONTINUOUS SOLUTION IMPROVEMENT PROGRAM

During the prior steps of the Business Development Process, a two-way exchange of information was the fundamental ingredient for successfully developing a fit between your company and the prospective customer. Instituting a continuous solution improvement program is simply a continuation of that information exchange.

Earlier in the Business Development Process, your staff's source of information from the prospective customer was information from interviews, surveys, industry information, and your company's history with similar types of customers. Now, along with monitoring those same sources, your staff will use your actual performance data gathered in delivering your service or product, staff experiences, customer business performance information, and other measureable types of information. All of this information will contribute to a continual analysis process, with the outcome being better solutions and an increasingly tighter fit between the two companies. Figure 21–1 demonstrates the continuous solution improvement process.

PROCESS DEFINITION

The process needs to be clearly defined by your company and a staff member assigned to coordinate each customer. The continuous solution improvement process uses information from the ongoing monitoring of the customer's needs and service requirements process discussed in the last chapter but goes far beyond it. This process is more strategic—looking for future opportunities; while the other is more pragmatic—solving day-to-day problems.

PERFORMANCE ASSESSMENT SURVEY

From the time your company is approved as a service or product provider, it should regularly administer a performance assessment survey. This survey will give the customer the opportunity to express their opinions of your company's service or product performance. By administering this on a regular basis, your staff will be able to chart trends over time. This is an important way to both root out potential problems and see potential opportunities.

The survey could contain whatever questions your staff feels contain information that needs to be rated depending on the needs and service requirements statement that was developed as part of the five-step monitoring process in the Approval step. The survey should at least ask the customer to rate the following:

➲ The performance of your company as a whole.

➲ How the solution your company proposed is meeting expectations.

➲ The performance of your company's specific service or product.

FIGURE 21-1   CONTINUOUS SOLUTION IMPROVEMENT PROCESS

Solution Improvement &
New Opportunities Process

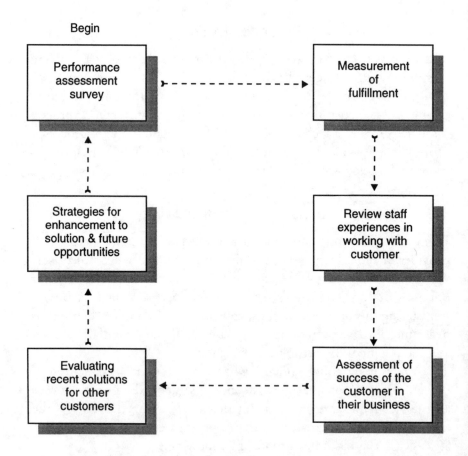

➲ How well your company has met the critical buying factor the customer established before your company was selected as an approved provider.

➲ How well your company's staff has performed according to the customer's expectations.

The performance assessment survey can take different forms. In fact, your staff may want to have several formats that can be administered at different times or to different representatives of the customer. One format might be a verbal interview that a customer service staff member performs in person. Another format might be a written survey that is sent to key customer personnel. A third format would be a focus group including both customer staff members as well as internal customers from within your company who are involved in fulfilling the customer's needs and service requirements.

Measurement of Fulfillment

This is a measurement of how well your company is meeting the needs and service requirements of the customer and should come directly from the five-step monitoring process in the Approval step.

Customer Business Performance Information

Another important element of this process is an assessment of the success of the customer in its own business. Sources for this type of information include business and trade publications; annual reports if the company is publicly held; and information gathered from your company's sales, marketing, or customer service staff. A careful eye on information that the customer makes public can often point out opportunities for future business. A current customer may have an article published about its plans to expand into new markets that may present your company with an increased opportunity with that customer.

Recent Experiences with Similar Types of Customers

Another area that is important to evaluate in looking for ways of improving solutions and future business opportunities is your company's recent experiences with other customers. This can come from new solutions developed to further a relationship with an existing customer or from a new solution developed to obtain business from a new prospective customer. Regular interviews with customer service staff may also reveal opportunities for improving solutions.

ANALYSIS AND STRATEGY FOR ENHANCEMENTS TO SOLUTION AND FUTURE OPPORTUNITIES

The final part to a successful continuous solutions improvement process is to have a team of staff members who can carry on the function of the strategy team in the Strategy step of the Business Development Process. Just like the strategy team, the members of this group will regularly look for ways to either improve existing solutions or create new solutions for future business opportunities that have been identified.

SUMMARY

Through the development and practice of these improvement processes, your company will be continuously finding ways to increase the benefits the customer recognizes from the business relationship. The following results should be realize:

For the customer:
➲ A lowering of the customer's overhead costs, or

➲ An increase in revenues from new sources.

For your company:
➲ An increase in profitable new business.

This will mean that a win-win situation exists for both your customer and your company. With this type of relationship, your customer can clearly see that your company's motivation is to find profitable ways to create value-added service or product solutions for both of you. The outcome of this will be to select your company as the preferred provider of your service or product. This is the objective of the Preferred step of the Business Development Process.

PART VII

THE NECESSARY ELEMENTS

Key Elements of Success

In the course of this book, you have learned the different elements of the Business Development Process. Like any process, its success is only as great as the effort put into it. To increase revenue using this system, a quality process must be instituted that monitors, measures, and modifies the Business Development Process. Instituting a quality process means setting specific goals and requirements for the Business Development Process, then following the process we have developed to match those goals and requirements. This final section outlines how to set up a quality management process. Figure 22–1 shows a quality management process model.

Establishing Requirements and Goals

The Business Development Process is made up of thirteen-steps to turn prospective customers into long-term customers. The purpose of this process is to create new profitable sources of sales revenue for your company. These are the requirements of your company's Business Development Process.

The amount of profitable sales revenue that will be necessary to establish as a goal will vary from company to company. Depending on the size of your company, the number of employees, funds available, and the time that can be dedicated, the amount of resources that your company has to invest into the Business Development Process will affect the goals you can reasonably set.

Figure 22–1 Quality Management Process to Monitor, Measure, and Modify Process

Quality Management
Process Model

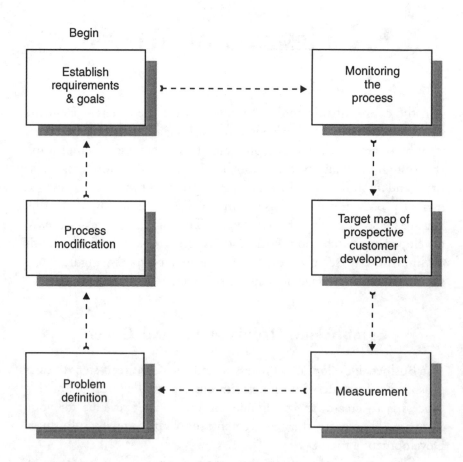

To establish a goal, begin by determining what you would consider a satisfactory result. In other words, if your company had already implemented the Business Development Process, what would be the desired outcome to consider the effort a success?

Next, you will need to establish what resources are necessary to achieve the satisfactory result. This will include determining the following:

- What marketing communications materials inventory can be utilized.

- New communication materials.

- The staff and time to dedicate to the process.

- Software or hardware your staff may want to utilize throughout the process.

- The commitment of management and other departments or staff involved in the process.

At this point, you will have to evaluate exactly what resources are available, then compare the difference between what you need to meet your goal and what you feel is actually available. If you feel there is a significant gap between the two, either adjust your goal accordingly or justify the additional resources to the appropriate source. It is important to remember that the Business Development Process can start off with a small effort, then expand as success is measured. This is especially true in the early use of the Business Development Process, because it may take you and your staff time to gain experience and establish what resources are necessary to meet your goal.

Once you have been able to establish your company's Business Development Process goal, be sure that everyone involved is aware of it. In addition, regularly update everyone involved with the progress that has been made in achieving the goal.

MONITORING THE PROCESS

To accurately determine the effectiveness of your Business Development Process, your staff will need an up-to-the-minute status report of where every prospective customer in your target prospect group is within the bull's-eye target model. At every step of the process, if prospective customers in the process are neglected, the timing of the process will be thrown off, earlier effort will be wasted, and the goals of the process will be unattainable.

PROSPECTIVE CUSTOMER TARGET MAP

To keep prospective customers from falling through the cracks, a visual tracking map can prove valuable. There are several ways of accomplishing this, but a prospective customer target map is particularly effective. The map is made up of a large graphic of the bull's-eye target. Within each ring, individual steps of the process that are a part of that ring must be defined. A graphic element with a numeric code for each prospective customer should then be attached to the target map. This can be accomplished manually, using a bulletin board with numerically coded pin flags, or by using a computer and graphic software such as Adobe Systems Incorporated's PageMaker or FreeHand, or Corel Systems Corporation's CorelDraw.

Figure 22–2 illustrates a prospective customer target map.

MEASUREMENT

Several measurements are essential to the Business Development Process. These types of measurements are: schedule conformance, quantitative prospective development, and sales revenue generated.

SCHEDULE CONFORMANCE

Schedule conformance is the measurement of the communication plan being completed on time. As each prospective customer reaches the Planning step, a strategic communication plan was produced. This plan should include specific target dates for each action to take place. To

Figure 22–2 Prospective Customer Target Map

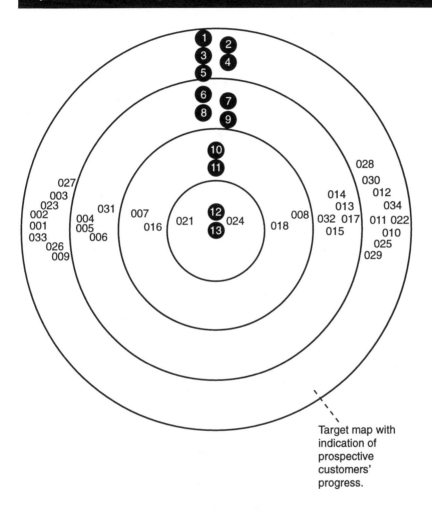

Target map with indication of prospective customers' progress.

Step 1—Target	001-ABC Company, 002-XYZ Company, 022-QWE Associates, 033-MNB Inc,
Step 2—Identification	003-LRF Partners, 010-DEF Corporation, 023-RTY Corporation, 034-ZXC Partners
Step 3—Introduction	011-UVW Inc, 012-MSG Corporation, 025-UIO Inc.
Step 4—Prequalification	027-HIJ Corporation, 028-RST Company, 026-PAS Partners
Step 5—Plan	029-ORH Company, 030-OPQ Inc, 009-DFG Corporation
Step 6—Awareness	004-GHI Inc, 005-LMN Company, 017-HJK Limited
Step 7—Knowledge	006-KLM Associates, 013-IJK Corporation
Step 8—Assessment	014-BGT Company, 015-MJU Inc,
Step 9—Proof	031-ZAQ Partners, 032-XSW Company
Step 10—Strategy	007-TGB Limited, 008-RFV Company
Step 11—Proposal	016-OPL Inc, 018-WSX Company
Step 12—Approval	021-RDX Company
Step 13—Preference	024-YHN Associates

manage the Business Development Process effectively, this measurement is important. If too many nonconformances to the planned schedule are recorded, your company's process for implementing the Business Development Process will have to be modified.

QUANTITATIVE PROSPECTIVE DEVELOPMENT

Quantitative prospect development is the measurement of the number of prospective customers that have reached different steps in the Business Development Process. This measurement is important to the management of the Business Development Process because it will demonstrate the accuracy and quality of your staff's selection of target prospect groups. As your staff selects different types of target market groups, either by size, location, or type of industry, these measurements will suggest future selections of target prospect groups.

SALES REVENUE GENERATED

Sales revenue is the measurement of revenue that has been received from new customers who have gone through the Business Development Process. This is the most absolute of all the measurements. All the other measurements will help your staff realize where and if modification to the process is necessary. This measurement will give your company an overall picture of the effectiveness of the Business Development Process. If more resources are desired for the process, this measurement can be the justification for it.

Modifying the Process

Monitoring and measuring of the Business Development Process will alert your company if your implementation process is not meeting the established requirements and goals. Should regular review of your company's monitoring and measurement signal that your process implementation is off course, you will need to modify your process. Modification of the process has two parts. The first is problem definition, and the second is the actual process modification.

Problem Definition

Before jumping in and modifying the implementation of your process, it is critical to clearly define where the problem exists. To accurately define the location of problems that monitoring or measurements have indicated, it is important to look deeper into the situation. This can best be done by analyzing the specific area of concern. A bubble diagram that illustrates the action steps of the area of concern should indicate where and what the problem is. For instance, your company is concerned that the strategic communication plans are not being executed according to the timeline. Measurement has indicated that 30 percent of the prospective customers are not receiving communication pieces as scheduled. A bubble diagram that illustrates the process of preparing mailings to prospective customers would indicate that there is a breakdown of the process between the person responsible for producing the schedule and the person who puts the information in the mail.

Process Modification

Once the problem has been clearly defined, attention can be directed to modifying the process. Process modification can be anything from a minor adjustment to a major change in the action steps your staff takes. If a major change is required, be sure to research what the best alternatives to solving the situation are. Next, determine the resources that will be needed to make the modification. If possible, test the modification to see if it will cause the necessary effects. Finally, implement the change to the process. Using our previous example, the modification might be that a check-off sheet needs to be sent from the person who produces the schedule to the person who puts the information in the mail. Or it may be determined that the same person who produces the schedule should also put information in the mail.

Conclusion

The purpose of this book has been to define a systematic process that will effectively grow a business in the changing economic environment.

The Business Development Process's thirteen-steps require your company to make a cost-effective investment of marketing and sales resources, with the end result producing maximum return on the investment—new profitable revenue sources. The key to the success of your company's implementation of the process will be a consistent effort to move prospective customers through the bull's-eye target model, finding a fit between your company and theirs that will produce a value-added benefit for the customer. With continuous monitors, measures, and modification of customer solutions, long-term win-win relationships will be your company's reward.

Best of luck!

Index

About the Author

David J. Rosenzweig is currently Director of Marketing for Lynden Air Freight in Seattle, WA, where he creates and coordinates the business development efforts targeted at major national accounts. He is a graduate of the University of Washington. For 10 years prior to his current position, Mr. Rosenzweig headed his own marketing communications consulting firm, working with leading Northwest corporations, including Microsoft Corporation, Weyerhaueser Recovery Services, and Safeco Insurance Company.